W9-AAM-843

Editor
Sara Connolly

Editorial Project Manager
Betsy Morris, Ph.D.

Editor-in-Chief
Sharon Coan, M.S. Ed.

Cover Artist
Brenda DiAntonis

Art Manager
Kevin Barnes

Creative Director
CJae Froshay

Imaging
Ralph Olmedo, Jr.
James Edward Grace

Product Manager
Phil Garcia

Publisher
Mary D. Smith, M.S. Ed.

BEST
Internet Activities
Second Edition

Teacher Created Resources, Inc.
6421 Industry Way
Westminster, CA 92683
www.teachercreated.com
ISBN-0-7439-3804-6
©2004 Teacher Created Resources, Inc.
Reprinted, 2005
Made in U.S.A.

Table of Contents

Introduction

An Introduction to the Internet 1
Using this Book 3
Class Management Tips 4
Classroom Benefits 5
Fitting It All In 6
Maximize Online Experiences 7
Internet Tips 8
Copyright Concerns 10
Unacceptable Material 11
Acceptable Use Policy 12
Safety Issues 13
Internet Safety Rules for Students 14
Parental Consent Form 15
Internet Wizard Award Form 15

Electronic Mail

Electronic Mail 16
"Keypal" 17
E-mail Rules 18
Writing E-mail in Style 19
E-mail mailing list 20

Using Search Engines

Using Search Engines 21
Search Engines, Directories, and Hybrid Engines 22
Defining Your Search 23
Ranking Search Engines 24
Refining Your Search 25
Search Engine Strategies 26

Language Arts

Groups 27
   Imaginative Minds 28
   The Presidents 31
   Native Americans 35
   Mathematicians 42
   The Vikings 46
   Web Tour Guides 49

Individuals 51
   Betsy Ross 52
   Alexander Graham Bell 56
   George Washington Carver 60

Table of Contents *(cont.)*

The Wright Brothers 63
Susan B. Anthony 66
Martin Luther King, Jr. 69
Jackie Robinson 73
Amelia Earhart 77
Charles Lindbergh 80
Explorers of the West 83

History 85
Immigration 86
The History of Aviation 90
The Olympics 94
Popcorn 98
The Ancient World 102

Places
United States 109
The 50 States 110
Alaska 113
Hawaii 117
Washington D.C. 121
Cross Country Tour 126
U.S. Geography 130
Virtual Field Trips 134

International 136
The Blarney Stone 137
Japan 141
Mexico: The Mayas 145
Africa: On Safari 150
China 155
Online Travel Log 159

Science and Natural Phenomena 163
Animals 164
Healthy Choices 168
Weather Browser 171
Scientists' Gazette 173
Going Buggy! 175
Love That Lava 179
Rain Forest Stations 182

Table of Contents *(cont.)*

Math 190
    What's Cooking? 191
    The Solar System 193
    Size is Relative 199
    The National Debt 205
    Flags of the Sea 210
    How Big is a Whale? 217
    Penny for Your Thoughts 226
    Finding Your Way 233
    We're Goin' Shoppin' 238

Art 240
    Online Museum Tour 241
    Origami Originals 244
    At the Circus 246

Holidays 250
    Chinese New Year 251
    Valentine's Day 255
    St. Patrick's Day 259
    Easter 263
    Halloween 267
    Thanksgiving 271
    Christmas Around the World 275

Collaborative Projects 279
    Online Book Reviews 280
    Collaborative Projects 282
    Partner Poems 288
    Cyberwriters Needed! 290
    Smarter Than the Average Textbook 292
    Lost: One Entire School 294
    Creating Class Bookmarks 296

Answer Key to Selected Exercises 299

Teacher Resource Sites 303

Introduction

What Is the Internet?

Much of today's correspondence is done electronically by e-mail, fax, computer database, and other means. People send and retrieve information efficiently with the use of a computer or other technologically advanced machines. The Internet provides information resources through the use of a network specifically designed for computers. The slice of information from the Internet viewed as text and graphics is called the World Wide Web. Other pieces of the Internet include bulletin board systems, chat rooms, and e-mail services. Internet users can "browse" Web sites for information, order tickets, ask questions of an expert, or do virtually anything one can imagine, all without having to get out from behind a desk. This "information superhighway" takes Internet users virtually anywhere they want to go at anytime. Travel to Alaska by Internet. Want to see the real thing? Use the Internet to book yourself a cruise!

The Internet is nothing more than a network of interconnected electronic data which crisscrosses and zigzags over miles and miles of phone line, creating a "web". After identifying a particular topic, one may access Web sites available on the Internet. These Web sites may be independent of one another or connect to related Web pages. Textual "links" are usually a different color from the normal text of the Web site. They may be purple or red words embedded in black text, for example. By clicking them, the Web page currently displayed connects to the next link. Links can also be graphic items (pictures). Anytime the cursor changes to a pointing hand, you know you have found a link.

How Do I Get There?

In order to explore the Internet, you will need four things: (1) a computer with Internet capabilities, (2) access to a network via a telephone line (an Internet service provider), (3) a Web browser such as *Netscape Communicator* or *Microsoft Internet Explorer*, and (4) a destination. Some online services such as America Online and Compuserv offer a network and Web browser all in one. This means that by launching the Internet icon, users automatically dial in to their network and view the Internet through their browser. Trouble may arise if you live in a remote area where there are no local access numbers to dial. In this situation, users not only pay the company for the use of their program but also pay long distance telephone fees. Many smaller (but local) Internet service providers have emerged to save Internet users huge phone bills. Check your local telephone directory and call (yes, with an actual telephone!) to set up access through a local Internet service provider's number. So far, these companies have been rather reasonable with their rates. You usually have a choice of limiting the number of calls you make, therefore limiting your Internet exploration time, or signing up for unlimited hours. This might be an option if you are considering downloading information and/or programs off the Net, which can sometimes take hours, depending on the size of the program. Check out what's available to you in your area, and then decide which method of logging on and browsing is right for you.

Important Information

Web sites frequently change addresses or become unavailable for myriad reasons. Teacher Created Resources attempts to offset this ongoing problem by posting changes of URLs on our Web site. For your convenience, we are providing active links to the Web sites listed for the activities in this book. No need to type in each Web site address. Simply bookmark our site for this book (**http://www.teachercreated.com/books/3804**) and click on the link(s) for the page of your lesson to go to the Web site(s).

So Many Destinations, So Little Time

Once you're safely logged on, the virtual world is at your fingertips! This can be a blessing or a curse. Once you start exploring on the "Information Superhighway," you will find that some roads are endless while others become a dead end. Some are toll roads, and others are bridges. Don't become discouraged your first time on the Net. If you make a wrong turn or end up in a deserted town, get back in that vehicle and press onward.

Take some time to just explore without a destination in mind. Get a feel for how the Web system works. Then try hunting for specific information on a particular subject. A host of popular search engines exist, such as Excite, Yahoo, and Infoseek, to name a few. Type in a topic of interest and let the engine search. The computer will access any and all sites and related categories that match the topic. You may find a need to narrow a search by typing in more specific information or broaden a search by typing in a more general subject.

Most search engine home pages list popular subject areas or categories with which to begin a search. Try one of these headings and see where it takes you. If it's not what you're looking for, you can always abort the mission and return to the home page. (An icon specifically for this task, labeled <Back>, is at the top of the taskbar.)

You've seen the advertisements for a company's Web site: http://www.(blah).com. This is called a URL or Uniform Resource Locator. Typing in an Internet address or URL at the top of the taskbar and striking the return key will launch you directly to that site.

Can I Ever Get Back?

You may find yourself easily lost if following a site that links to one page after another on related topics. Make a bookmark of the site's home page before going on so that if you do make a wrong turn but want to keep exploring this site, you won't have to go back ten links to find the original page.

One may assume that no one has ever disappeared while exploring the Internet. It's not the Bermuda Triangle, although it may seem so to new users. A more accurate metaphor is a maze with many rooms. When you first enter, you're still fairly safe. But as you move from room to room, it becomes trickier to retrace your steps. Fortunately, a safety line is always near.

The Internet works like any other computer program. When you're ready to quit, simply exit or quit the program. If you're online with a network separate from your browser, be sure to disconnect the phone connection. If disconnection is forgotten, the computer will stay online even though you're off to the grocery store. And this will use up valuable time with the Internet service provider while blocking the phone line to incoming (and outgoing) calls.

Using This Book

The activities in this book and related sites were picked because they represented a wide variety of topics, user levels, and a broad spectrum of exercises that can be done using sites on the World Wide Web. Use the lesson plans as they exist or modify them to reflect your curriculum and students' education level.

Be sure to access the focus Web site (or destination URL) before engaging students in the activity. Web sites tend to change over time, and you don't want to meet with any surprises while browsing live with the class. If for some reason the Web site listed is no longer available, try one of the alternate URLs. Many of the focus sites in this guide are actually links or links within links of a home page. An arrow or icon may be at the bottom indicating "Go Back." If interested, link to view the original site of the focus Web site. But once again, be sure to preview it before using it with the class.

Become familiar with the students' responsibilities for each task. See "Classroom Management Tips" for more details on how to go about engaging all the students in active Internet learning.

Begin the lesson with the suggested pre-Internet activity. Access the destination URL, and be prepared to help the students obtain information as they participate in this high-tech research. After the students have completed their online investigation and Internet activity, try one or all of the "Extended Activities" designed to supplement the focus activity.

Students will need about twenty to thirty minutes to complete the actual online activity. Plan to spend additional time preparing or reviewing with the class during the pre-Internet and extended activities.

The focus Web sites were chosen because of their age-level appropriateness for primary students. Still, some of the textual information may be too difficult for some students to read independently. Students may need assistance when reading the text.

None of the activities calls for e-mailing or visiting a chat group. E-mailing takes a day or two. E-mailers send a message and then the person who received the message responds. You may wish to e-mail the author or company responsible for a particular Web site to tell them how much the class enjoyed it, what they learned, etc. Chat groups are an instantaneous transfer of typed messages. Since you cannot control what others may write and, thus, what the students may read, this act of information exchange is not recommended. There are plenty of honest, wholesome, kid-related chat groups out there, but this guide is intended to help students use the Internet to gather information, not chat with a person they've never met.

Note: The materials list at the beginning of each chapter does not include supplies for the extended lessons.

Classroom Management

The activities in this guide assume that the students have one computer in their classroom with Internet access. Allocate the use of the Internet to ensure that all students have equitable experience on the Net in one of several ways. Some of the activities have instructions to launch the focus Web site as a class. Others suggest grouping the students and allowing them to take turns. Regardless of the instructions for the individual activities, adapt them to suit the needs of your classroom.

To Launch a URL with the Whole Class

If this is the method of choice, or if the activity calls for it, try attaching an overhead projector or television monitor to the computer if it has these capabilities. This will allow for easier viewing by the entire class. Make sure all the students have a copy of the activity page so they can follow along. Keep everyone on task by rotating volunteers to click at the site and read portions of the information.

Working in Groups

Another option is to have the students work in small groups to access the desired Web page(s). First, provide a whole-class lesson demonstration of how to accomplish this. For occasions when you may not be directly available, elicit the help of an adult volunteer to make sure the students are typing in the exact URL, following the directions on the activity sheet, obtaining the information necessary for successful completion of the activity, and avoiding the temptation of downloading or e-mailing. Volunteers may be coworkers, parent volunteers, administrators, or perhaps a school media specialist or technology teacher. Even if some students have prior experience using the Internet, be sure to provide them with the support they may need to successfully read the information and complete the activity pages.

One way to manage Internet groups effectively is to have the Internet activity as a rotation center. This way, all the students are engaged in a meaningful project while you help those on the Internet, and all the groups will have a turn on the Internet.

Save It for Later!

A final option is to save the sites for easier access unless the students are to practice typing in the exact URL. (See "Internet Tips" for information about *Web Whacker*, bookmarks, and saving the file.)

Classroom Benefits

By using the Internet in your classroom, you and your students will be able to:

- go directly to the best source

- explore other peoples' ideas

- facilitate collaborative learning

- use telementoring selectively

- exchange information throughout the world

- locate and retrieve timely information as needed for your classroom

- access multimedia sources which would otherwise not be available to you

- access real-world data and information contained in various databases

- publish your works immediately

- reach larger audiences

- add a variety of instructional strategies

- expand and enhance communication opportunities

- experience success in learning to do research

- find a vast amount of instructional materials for use in your classroom

- prepare for inevitable future changes in our world

- convert your classroom into an information resource center in which you collect and share data with each other.

Fitting It All In

You will find the Internet useful to enhance your curriculum relating to various topics through the lessons supplied for you in this book. The lessons include teaching objectives, materials needed, Web Sites, general information on the topic, specific steps for teaching the lesson, related activity sheets, suggested student projects, and extended activities along with other sites to explore.

Give yourself enough time to feel comfortable with the materials and the World Wide Web environment before you do a Web activity with your students or start an online project. In other words, make haste slowly!

The Internet is a good place for
- locating information not available in textbooks or the classroom/school library
- finding and contacting experts in a particular subject area
- utilizing government information which is not easily accessible outside of the Internet to the general public
- sharing information with other teachers and/or students from anywhere in the world
- publishing students' work online
- obtaining timely information (breaking news)
- reducing professional isolation by helping teachers keep in contact with professional colleagues worldwide
- helping students retain material
- gaining maximum educational value with limited time commitment.

The Internet is not a good place to
- find summaries or quick overviews of a topic
- replace hands-on activities such as drawing, writing, building, etc., although it can supplement these activities
- have active face-to-face interaction with other students and teachers.

Maximize the Experiences

1. Ideally, the computer and phone line for Internet access should be within your classroom so you can monitor and assist students' activities while they are online.

2. Set up several activities to do within a specific time frame so students can move on to another activity if a server is down or the site is temporarily unavailable due to heavy traffic, weather, etc. (You should not be online during a thunder and lightning storm since it could damage your equipment. Usually the phone lines are not as reliable and your connection may be broken.)

3. Do a preliminary check on intended sites as close as possible to the intended time of day to determine if they are usually available at that time. Access is becoming more of a problem as students' use of the Internet increases.

4. Always give students some type of written response sheet to indicate how they spent their time online, or have them provide information about sites they visited.

5. Combine online with offline activities, particularly if you have limited access to an Internet connection.

6. Whenever possible, instruct students to turn off the automatic graphics loading option in their browser, or, if written materials are what you are most interested in viewing, have them select the text-based option if it is available at a site.

7. Providing you have a reasonably good, fast printer, consider printing out necessary information and viewing it offline.

8. Consider allowing students to do the assignment during another time of day, after or before school hours or at home if they have Internet access.

9. Remember that careful planning prior to doing an online project with students will greatly enhance your chances for a successful experience.

10. Plan enough exploratory time. These activities take more time than teacher-directed activities. Without enough time, students will feel frustrated and will find it difficult to stay on task.

11. Allow students to work in groups since this lets them share ideas, resources and tools.

12. Keep students focused and actively involved with the objectives of the activity by periodically asking them questions about the information they are finding:

    Is this information accurate and helpful in achieving the learning goal?

    Is all the information available at this site or do we need to look further?

    What should we do with the information we have found?

Internet Tips

- Know the exact URL or have a specific topic in mind to investigate.

- Type in the Uniform Resource Locator (http://). This includes all letters, numbers, punctuation, and symbols. Just like an address, sending a package to an incorrect postal address will result in a "return to sender" message.

- When conducting a topical search on the Internet typing in a series of words for which to search will instruct the Search engine to link all those words individually. Put quotation marks around the words that act as one topic (e.g., "Native Americans" or "United States Geography").

- Be patient when downloading sites with bountiful graphics as they take up a lot of computer memory. Large graphics may take some time to fully "develop," depending on the speed of the modem and other uncontrollable factors. Try visiting the site and connecting to all the links prior to engaging the class. When you return to the same site within a reasonable amount of time, the computer will have held some graphic information in memory. This will accelerate downloading time.

- Many persons or organizations with Web sites have encouraged businesses to advertise on their page(s). Be on the look out for links to advertisements and learn to ignore them (unless they are promoting something in which you may have an interest). Teach students to do the same. If you accidentally link to an advertisement, click the **<Back>** arrow at the top of the taskbar to return to the previous page.

- Text portions of Web sites usually arrive much more quickly than accompanying graphics. Arrow down the page and read the text while the graphics are downloading. Then arrow back up the page and view the artwork and pictures.

- Murphy's Law definitely applies anytime you wish to incorporate technology in the classroom. Expect things to go wrong, even after careful planning. If a Web site is unavailable or your ISP line is busy, have an alternate project ready for the students to complete. If the computer displays a "return to sender" message, double-check to be sure you typed in the exact URL.

- A software program called *Web Whacker* by Blue Squirrel is ideal for classroom surfing. This program allows users to download an entire Web site onto the hard drive or zip drive. Users may also select the number of levels (or links) to include. Then the students need only launch the file name of the saved information to complete the activities. Although students won't actually be "on the Net," the information is viewed as if they really were, and their interaction is censored by guaranteeing they can't e-mail or download programs.

- Another option is to bookmark the sites. (Click **<Bookmark>** from the taskbar and drag down to **<Add a Bookmark>**.) When students go online, they only need to click and drag to the correct bookmark; they will automatically be transported to the focus Web site.

- Another way to save sites is by selecting **<File...Save As>**. Choose a drive to save the site and give it an appropriate file name. A word of caution, though. Saving Web sites will only save the text portion (no graphics), and some sites won't save at all. (They look like computer script when the file is opened). A final option is to simply print the site.

- The information age is here to stay (at least for a while), but some parents may be uncomfortable with their children's access to the Internet. Before beginning any Internet projects, have parents sign the consent form on page 15.

- Check out Web sites before allowing students to go online. Although the Web sites in this guide were consulted beforehand, some sites may have changed, been moved, or somehow incorporated information not appropriate for young students. If this is the case, do some investigative research on your own to find a suitable Web page for the class. Some reliable and user-friendly search engines are listed on the following page.

- Have a question about a site? Click on FAQ (frequently asked questions) to see if others have wondered the same thing. If your question isn't spotlighted at this link, as least you'll learn information you hadn't thought to ask. E-mail the creator of a site to beg for the answers to the most burning questions or to express your thanks for providing a most educational Internet opportunity for students. Most creators are quick with their responses; they usually write back by the next day.

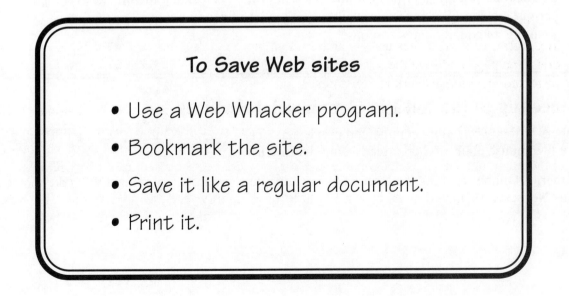

To Save Web sites

- Use a Web Whacker program.
- Bookmark the site.
- Save it like a regular document.
- Print it.

Copyright Concerns

Because the Internet is a somewhat new medium in the public's hands, there are several gray areas surrounding copyright. However, "Gee, your honor! There are so many gray areas!" is no defense if someone ever chooses to sue you or your school for playing fast and loose with intellectual property.

By the time you read this, there should be some clearer guidelines on copyright, but in case there are not, here are some that might help (with assistance from the founder of ClariNet, Brad Templeton, and his *Ten Big Myths About Copyright Explained*).

1. Almost everything is copyrighted the minute it is written. No copyright notice is required.

2. As much as possible, your students should paraphrase and give attribution. (That is solid writing practice anyway.)

3. Whether you charge money or not, you can still violate someone's copyright.

4. E-mail and material posted in newsgroups and on bulletin boards are still protected. Whether you or other authors want to make an issue out of protected material is for another forum.

5. What about fair use? This is a concept/term schools often turn to for guidance. Basically, keep it short and give attribution. Use only what is necessary to make your point.

6. Do not assume that by using others' material that you are helping to promote original work. The author may, in fact, appreciate it, but he/she will appreciate it more if you ask permission. Besides, he/she may have valid reasons for not granting permission.

7. What about photographs, online graphics from Web pages, and drawings/diagrams? Elementary school students cannot always go around clipping pictures (including the credits) out of encyclopedias and the latest new magazines. On the up side, asking permission from Web sites is usually just a matter of sending a quick e-mail message and awaiting an equally quick response.

Connecting to the Net Via Commercial Services

Members of the two leading commercial online services—America Online (AOL) and Prodigy—need only a few mouse clicks to hop directly onto the Internet.

On America Online, clicking the Internet Connection button on the main menu will take members to the various Net services, including their own World Wide Web browser.

Unacceptable Material

One of the biggest issues surrounding educational use of the Internet in schools is the question of acceptable use. There are many sites on the Internet which are unsuitable for viewing by children. The fear that students will access unacceptable material has limited the use of the Internet in some schools. To alleviate this problem, many school districts have developed an acceptable use policy which outlines the responsibilities of the individual user whenever he or she uses an Internet connection.

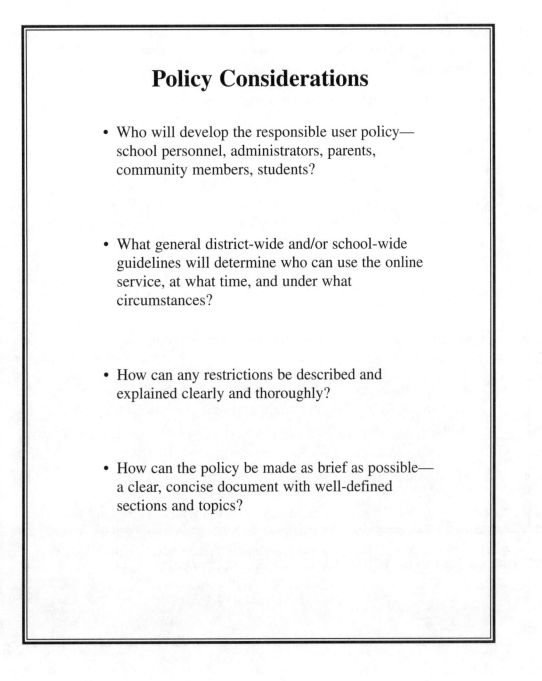

Policy Considerations

- Who will develop the responsible user policy—school personnel, administrators, parents, community members, students?

- What general district-wide and/or school-wide guidelines will determine who can use the online service, at what time, and under what circumstances?

- How can any restrictions be described and explained clearly and thoroughly?

- How can the policy be made as brief as possible—a clear, concise document with well-defined sections and topics?

Acceptable Use Policy

In developing an Acceptable Use Policy:

- consider first adherence to any current local, state, or federal laws

- provide a description of the limitations of access, if any

- define authorized use and authorized access

- explain the responsibilities of anyone accessing the Internet through school facilities. This can include parent, students, teachers, support staff, groups meeting at the school, etc.

- define penalties for not abiding by the policies

- identify who can grant or revoke the privileges of net access

- provide information - particularly to students - about revealing personal information via the Internet or about meeting online acquaintances in person

- add signature lines for all users.

Once the policy is developed and ready to be implemented, be sure the information is shared with school personnel, community members, and anyone else who will be using the Internet. Copies should be distributed throughout the school and in appropriate information locations.

Safety Issues

Realize that the Internet is a neutral medium—culturally, racially, physically and with regard to gender. This can be an advantage to your students. However, the Internet has a dark side. It is also morally blind, making no judgements on what it passes on to the classroom screen. All you will know about the author of the data, or the other person you are communicating with, is what they reveal to you through the written message on the screen.

Just as we inform students about safety issues in dealing with strangers and potentially harmful situations outside the school, so too, we must let students know that there are some basic rules for online safety as well. The set of rules on page 14 was developed by the National Center for Missing and Exploited Children (1-800-THE-LOST) and the Interactive Services Association. They are included in a pamphlet entitled: "Child Safety on the Information Highway."

Since many of the activities available on the Internet can be done outside of school hours, parents will need to assume supervision of their children's use of the Internet. Many districts have a form that parents are required to sign indicating that they know the school's policy on general computer usage and Internet use specifically. A meeting with parents would also be appropriate—especially if you intend to do some kind of online project with your class. Getting parental cooperation is an important component for any successful Internet experience.

Tips for Teachers

- Supervise students while they are online.

- If it is difficult to keep students away from unacceptable sites, consider creating your own list of sites and allowing the students to visit only these sites.

- Monitor e-mail communications. If someone sends you or one of your students an obscene or suggestive e-mail with the intent to harass or threaten, report this to the National Center for Missing and Exploited Children's CyberTipline at 1-800-843-5678 or **www.missingkids.com/cybertip**.

- Use an Internet filtering program or service such as Cyber Patrol, Bess, CYBERsitter, or Safe Net Plus. Note however, that it is not safe to assume a filter will block all inappropriate sites. Supervision is still necessary.

- Note the sites that students are visiting and periodically view them yourself to confirm that they are acceptable.

- Require students to obtain your permission before downloading anything off the Internet.

And in the interest of protecting yourself and your students…

- NEVER send confidential information over the Internet, including information about a student to a parent. Assume that any e-mail you send can be read by anyone on the Internet who has the tools and knowledge to access your e-mail.

Internet Safety
Rules for Students

1. **I will not give out personal information** such as my address, telephone number, parents' work number or address, or the name and location of my school without my parents' permission.

2. **I will tell my parents right away** if I come across any information that makes me feel uncomfortable.

3. **I will never agree to get together with someone I "meet" online** without first checking with my parents. If my parents agree to the meeting, I will be sure that it is in a public place and bring my mother or father along.

4. **I will never send a person my picture** or anything else without first checking with my parents.

5. **I will not respond to any negative messages** that are mean or in any way make me feel uncomfortable. It is not my fault if I get a message like that. If I do, I will tell my parents right away so they can contact the online service.

6. **I will talk with my parents so that we can set up rules for going online.** We will decide upon the time of day I can be online, the length of time I can be online, and the appropriate areas for me to visit. I will not access other areas or break the rules without their permission.

Dear Parents,

We are fortunate to provide the most current electronic resources for our students. With your permission, our class will be exploring the Internet to gather valuable information related to various topics throughout the year. Please note that we will not be visiting "chat" rooms. All of the Internet sites have been previewed and deemed suitable for young learners. Each Internet activity will be supervised by an adult. At no time will the students be allowed to have free access to the Internet.

Please sign this form to grant permission for your child to use Internet resources and return it to school. We welcome you to join us one day to experience this extraordinary opportunity (days and times to be determined). Thank you for supporting our efforts to provide the most exciting educational opportunity for our students!

Sincerely,

_____ I give my child _____ permission to work on the Internet.

_____ I **DO NOT** wish my child to work on the Internet

Signed: _____

Congratulations!

This Award is to Certify That

_____

Is an Internet Wizard!

Signed: _____

Date: _____

Electronic Mail

As our world becomes more technologically-oriented, e-mail and other forms of electronic information transfer will become an accepted way of communicating. E-mail is already gaining acceptance as a way of transferring information among schools and students. In the world of business, advertising, and contact with associates via e-mail is commonplace. For students, even sending messages to their friends or relatives is instructional.

There are a number of curriculum-related activities that you can do with e-mail. For instance, you can get answers to questions about academic subjects, research topics for class reports, or just get another person's (or classroom's) perspective on a particular topic. In addition to learning about our own United States, you can explore and begin to appreciate differences in other societies, cultures, and countries. Personal connections made through e-mail can help you and your students broaden their viewpoints on any number of issues.

Some other examples of projects are

- analyzing stereotypes held by people in different areas of the world

- analyzing drinking water from a variety of sources

- writing myths from different cultures

- learning how holidays are celebrated around the world

- learning about money in different parts of the world

- exploring climates

Many sites on the Internet currently offer free e-mail accounts. If you would like each student in the class to have his or her own e-mail account, your best bet might be to sign up at one of these sites. You may have to put up with some advertising, but it will be worth it for the time you save.

E-mail offers a number of potential activities which are relevant to the social studies curriculum. The first thing you as a teacher need to do is to locate "keypals" or "penpals" for your students. Some sources for such projects, as well as classrooms and individuals wishing to correspond with others, can be found here:

http://www.teachercreated.com/books/3804

Click on page 16, sites 1, 2, 3, 4, 5

"Keypal"

Using e-mail in a "Keypal" activity is one of the least complicated activities you can use on the Internet. However, a successful student activity depends upon careful and thorough advance planning. Keypal's most common problem is too much unstructured time. To encourage students to stay on task, design a specific evaluation form (see below) to fit your needs.

A keypal activity is appropriate as an instructional strategy if you want to:

- connect students with an expert or mentor on a particular field

- practice a foreign language or learn about another culture or geographic location

- communicate information on relevant topics quickly

- learn how to write the researched information in a clear concise manner.

WEEKLY STUDENT EVALUATION

Project Title_____

Partners' Names_____

Starting Date/Time _____/_____**Completion Date/Time** _____/_____

Keypal name _____ **Total Time Online** _____

Goals_____

Description of Activity_____

_____

_____

Questions That Arose _____

_____

_____

Problems Encountered _____

_____

Solutions to Problems_____

_____

E-mail Rules

Prior to starting an e-mail activity, students should be made aware of some general rules and information about using e-mail properly and efficiently. One of the best sources for this is *The Net: User Guidelines and Netiquette* by Arlene H. Rinaldi. You can get a copy of this publication and other useful information on using e-mail at:

http://www.teachercreated.com/books/3804

Click on page 18, site 1

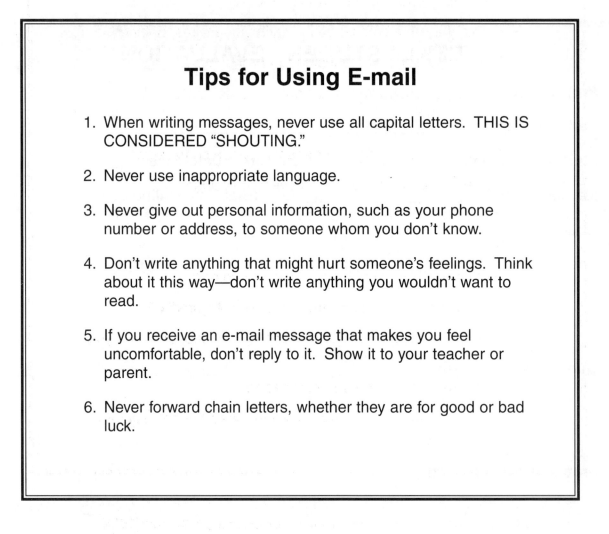

Tips for Using E-mail

1. When writing messages, never use all capital letters. THIS IS CONSIDERED "SHOUTING."

2. Never use inappropriate language.

3. Never give out personal information, such as your phone number or address, to someone whom you don't know.

4. Don't write anything that might hurt someone's feelings. Think about it this way—don't write anything you wouldn't want to read.

5. If you receive an e-mail message that makes you feel uncomfortable, don't reply to it. Show it to your teacher or parent.

6. Never forward chain letters, whether they are for good or bad luck.

Writing E-mail

Writing good e-mail messages is somewhat different than writing letters. Because the messages are usually short or you are sending a reply to a previously-received message, there are style issues you need to think about.

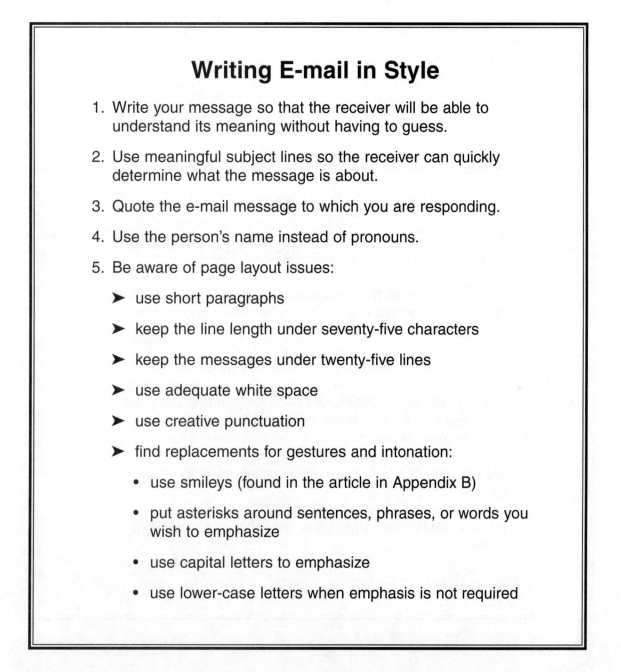

Writing E-mail in Style

1. Write your message so that the receiver will be able to understand its meaning without having to guess.

2. Use meaningful subject lines so the receiver can quickly determine what the message is about.

3. Quote the e-mail message to which you are responding.

4. Use the person's name instead of pronouns.

5. Be aware of page layout issues:

   ➤ use short paragraphs

   ➤ keep the line length under seventy-five characters

   ➤ keep the messages under twenty-five lines

   ➤ use adequate white space

   ➤ use creative punctuation

   ➤ find replacements for gestures and intonation:

      • use smileys (found in the article in Appendix B)

      • put asterisks around sentences, phrases, or words you wish to emphasize

      • use capital letters to emphasize

      • use lower-case letters when emphasis is not required

For additional information on this subject, read the article, "A Beginner's Guide to Effective E-mail" which can be found at: **http://www.teachercreated.com/books/3804**
Click on page 19, site 1

E-mail Mailing Lists

One common way to get information from other people about a particular topic is to join a mailing list or listserv. Here individuals can post messages, and other readers can respond. If the list is unmoderated, anything goes. There is no "quality control." Moderated mailing lists have already been filtered before they are released to the general list subscribers.

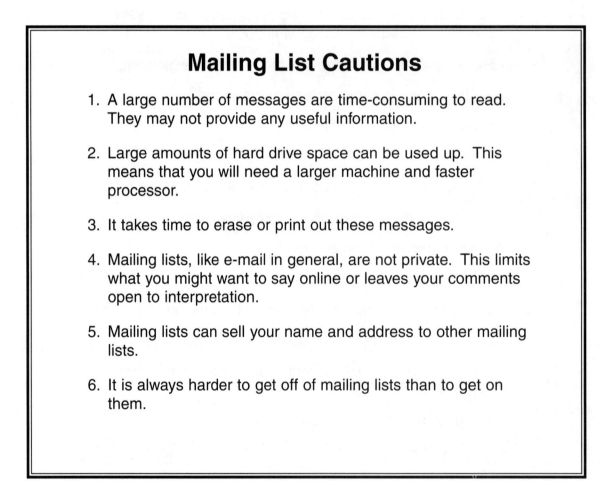

Mailing List Cautions

1. A large number of messages are time-consuming to read. They may not provide any useful information.

2. Large amounts of hard drive space can be used up. This means that you will need a larger machine and faster processor.

3. It takes time to erase or print out these messages.

4. Mailing lists, like e-mail in general, are not private. This limits what you might want to say online or leaves your comments open to interpretation.

5. Mailing lists can sell your name and address to other mailing lists.

6. It is always harder to get off of mailing lists than to get on them.

✸ ✸ ✸ Using Search Engines ✸ ✸ ✸

The ever-changing nature of the Internet means that Web sites disappear or change addresses all the time. There are some strategies that you can use when this situation presents itself so that you will know if the website you want is gone or has simply moved. This page details how to find out using URL strategies and search engines.

You'll Know a Web Site Address Isn't Working When...

- It is taking an extra long time to load the page.

- You receive an error page instead of the page you are looking for.

What to do if a Web Site Address Doesn't Work

- Check to make sure you typed the address EXACTLY as it appears, with all the characters (such as _, ~, //, etc.).

- Click the **Refresh** button at the top of your screen

- Enter the address again

- Type only the address of the home page and navigate from there. For example, if the address http://www.teachercreated.com/cgi-bin/urlsearch.cgi?2187 doesn't work, try truncating it to become: http://www.teachercreated.com. Then, click the links on the home page to find the specific Web page you are looking for. In some cases, the Web site will have a search engine in which you can type a keyword and find what you are looking for.

Using Keywords to Search

For example, if you want to visit a site called "Games Kids Play," and the address you have listed for the site is http://www.corpcomm.net/~gnieboer/gamehome.htm

you may find that when you type in the URL, you get a "page not found" message. You can then go to Google.com and type "Games Kids Play" (including quotation marks) in the search box. On the results page you will find the new URL for the site,

http://www.gameskidsplay.net

You can search using any information that you have for a site. In the example above, if you know the name of a type of game listed on the site, such as "circle games," you could include that information in your search, and on the results page you will most likely find a link that will take you directly to the circle games listed on that site.

Note: Web sites and Web pages are different things. A Web site usually consists of multiple Web pages, with a home page and several pages linked to the home page viewable by clicking buttons on the home page. A Web page is a single page, such as a home page or a linked page.

🔍 🕸 🔍 🕸 Using Search Engines *(cont.)* 🕸 🔍 🔍

Imagine glistening spider webs spiraling from your computer with information web sites at each junction of the silken threads. See tiny train engines, propelling themselves on spidery legs, racing from site to site, searching out the most relevant information on your topic. This ridiculous but visual cartoon illustrates the concept of search engines.

Search Engines, Directories, and Hybrid Engines

Most search engines include a help section providing information about unique features and capabilities of that engine. Get acquainted with several search engines and directories in order to switch from one to another when access and response comes more slowly during the daytime hours. Study the chart below to see the advantages and disadvantages of each.

Search engines, sometimes called "crawlers" or "spiders," are constantly visiting and indexing Internet web sites, voraciously searching and often finding information that is not listed in directories. The most well-known, commercially-backed search engines, are usually well-maintained, dependable, and frequently updated to keep up with the ever-growing web. They include such names as **Alta Vista, Excite, HotBot, Infoseek, Google, Lycos, Yahoo, Yahooligans, and WebCrawler.**

Subject directories are created by humans; therefore you may get better results from them. Instead of searching out information sites, directories categorize sites that are submitted to them. **Yahoo** is probably the best-known directory.

Hybrid search engines have an associated directory of sites that have been reviewed or rated available to users who ask to see the reviews.

SEARCH ENGINES	SUBJECT DIRECTORIES
* require more knowledge from the user * can be time-consuming * robot-driven index maintained by the computer * best for specific information * computer controls the searching pattern * can produce excessive results or "hits" if keywords are not well defined * keyword searchable * easy time saver for beginning web surfers	* sources preselected and index maintained by an expert in the field * focus is narrowed to relevant topics * keyword search allows more user control of the searching pattern * fixed vocabulary selected from established categories * sometimes contain keyword searches (not as capable as search engines)

✿ ✿ ✿ Defining Your Search ✿ ✿ ✿

Effective use of keywords is one way that beginning surfers can define and narrow their search parameters. All search engines begin with some type of dialog box which allows you to type in a keyword or phrase.

With some engines, you can also select a boolean operator (see page 25) or customize your search by defining other parameters such as time periods or location.

The first step is to define the topic and the type of information you want to find as specifically as possible. Once you have identified the topic/content, you can choose appropriate keywords for your search. A diagram of this process is shown below.

Preparing for a Keyword Search

Define the Topic: _____

Identify Search Objective: _____

Choose a Search Engine or Directory: _____

Define type of information as general or specific: _____

Define Keywords:

keyword one	keyword two	keyword three	keyword four
_____	_____	_____	_____
_____	_____	_____	_____
_____	_____	_____	_____
_____	_____	_____	_____

Before you begin an online search, list the keywords you intend to use. Include possible synonyms for your topic. Since thinking of synonyms is sometimes difficult while you are online, it is important to do this ahead of time. Many newer search engines, such as Infoseek, list related topic areas to help you in the search process. However, this does not help if you are searching for a very specific item within a particular topic area.

✸ ✸ Ranking Search Engines ✸ ✸

After trying several search engines, you can begin to make some judgments on which engine will work best for you. Knowing the features of each engine will help you make a better choice. The first consideration is the number of web pages and/or databases that are searched by the engine.

The real "acid test" for a search engine is not how many results they find but how many relevant sites they find. How a search engine "hits" (finds the matches) will often determine the relevancy of a particular result. This is influenced by where the engine looks for your keywords. An engine can search for keywords in a title, URL, the first 25 lines, or in the body of a document. Depending upon the database, you might miss a good site if the search engine does not look deep enough.

Different Methods of Ranking Results Used by Different Engines

Once the results are obtained, many engines use a ranking system to indicate how close the engine thinks a result is to the keyword(s) you have used. In this case, you will need to know how results are ranked. A ranking for a site is usually indicated by a percentage. Not all rankings are determined in the same way. **Yahoo**, a subject directory, determines their rankings in this way:

1. The highest ranking goes to the sites which match the most keywords.

2. Documents which have the keywords in the title are ranked higher than those which have the keywords in the body of the document or in the URL address.

3. The higher up the match in the category tree used by Yahoo, the higher the ranking.

Google is currently the most popular search engine on the Internet. Here's how Google determines their ranking:

1. each link a page receives counts as a "vote" for the site, which increases its rank in the results (Google also looks at the importance of the site the link comes from.)

2. text-matching techniques determine the importance of the text on the page and relevance to the search

3. Google goes beyond the number of times a term appears on the page and examines the page content.

Another popular search tool is **Infoseek**. This is really a hybrid search engine and subject directory since it has components of both. Their ranking percentage is called a "confidence level" with the most relevant matches appearing at the top of the list. Scoring is influenced by:

1. how near the beginning of a document the keywords are found (includes title)

2. the frequency of the keywords in the document

3. whether the keywords are "uncommon" and thus receive more weight in database.

Knowing how different search tools gather and report information can help you determine which engine is best for you. You will still need to spend time experimenting with different tools to determine which one(s) gives you the most relevant results for your needs.

✺ ✺ ✺ Refining Your Search ✺ ✺ ✺

After you have done a keyword search, you may find that the information is not exactly what you wanted. This usually happens because you have not used keywords which are specific. Most search engines include a section on searching tips which can help you do more efficient searches. One frequently-used way of narrowing your search is to use boolean operators. These are similar to those used in mathematical logical expressions. Since all search engines do not use operators in the same way, or they may include the NOT operator, be sure to check how the operators are used in any online search engine you use. It is important to know how each one affects the results since they will not always be the same.

In many of the newer search engines, the actual boolean operators are not used. Instead, you may be given choices which have the same effect and meaning. For instance, a choice which indicates that a search will be done on "all the words" is equivalent to the AND operator. If, on the other hand, you select "any of the words", you will get many more results since this is equivalent to using the OR operator. The most limiting choice would be to use a PHRASE option which will only search for a sequence of words. Since the phrase option greatly limits your results, you will sometimes get an empty list.

Summary of Boolean Operators

Operator	Equivalent	Best Used For
And	all the words	narrowing the results within a specific topic/content area
Or	any of the words	browsing for large amounts of information
Phrase	all the words in the exact sequence of the phrase	specific results within a well-defined topic/content area
Not	(no equivalent)	eliminating possible double meanings for keywords

✷ ✷ Search Engine Strategies ✷ ✷

The effective use of appropriate search strategies and engines will greatly improve your results and reduce your time online. Some general tips to consider are:

1. Understand the difference between search engines and subject directories. Know when to use each one.

2. Try different search engines and be sure to read the "tips or help" sections.

3. When using a search engine, plan your search ahead of time and be as specific as possible.

4. If the search engine has a rating system (usually expressed as a percentage), select those results with a 90% or above rating since they are more likely to contain the information you are seeking. (If you have the time, you might want to look at the other addresses and descriptions as well since a good address might appear further down the list.)

5. Use double quotes (" ") to indicate a phrase so the search will look for that "group" of words.

6. If a word must appear in the results, put a plus (+) in front of it.

7. If you don't want a word to appear in the results, put a (-) in front of it.

8. Learn to use "wildcards" which allow you to search for strings of words or for differences of spelling within words. (Wom*n will find woman, women).

9. Use boolean operators to broaden or limit your search.

In the next section, you will find several activities which you can use with your students to develop and reinforce their understanding of World Wide Web searching tools and strategies.

Language Arts

Groups

Imaginative Minds

The Presidents

Native Americans

Mathematicians

The Vikings

Web Tour Guides

✿ ✿ ✿ Imaginative Minds ✿ ✿ ✿

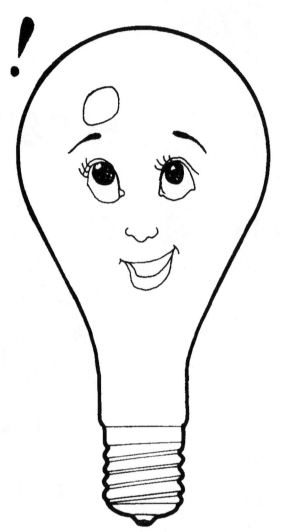

Objective:

Students use what they learned about inventors past and present to create unique and relevant inventions of their own which they display at a class "Invention Convention."

Materials Needed:

- one large cardboard box
- miscellaneous craft supplies
- note cards
- one copy of page 30 per team of students
- handy "junk" (bathroom tissue tubes, foil, cans, yarn, two-liter containers, shoeboxes, craft sticks, cotton, colored plastic wrap, etc.)

Web Sites:

http://www.teachercreated.com/books/3804

Click on page 28, sites 1, 2, 3, 4, 5

Keywords for Search Engines:

Using your favorite search engine (such as **Google.com**), type keywords "inventor," "invention," "patent process," or the name of an inventor.

Pre-Internet Activities:

- Teach the students about the process of applying for a patent. (The site entitled "U.S. Patent Process" is a good place to start.) Then allow teams of students to use their Internet research skills to discover some inventions people have created and patented. Discuss the motivation these inventors had for their creations and the math and science skills that were necessary before they began creating.

- Before investigating inventors of the past, have a small group of students create an "invention machine," using a large cardboard box and miscellaneous craft supplies. While learning about inventions by the famous inventors that follow, write the names of the inventions and their inventors (and perhaps the year they were created) on note cards. Place them in the "invention machine." See the first post-Internet activity below to find out what to do next.

Post-Internet Activities:

- After the students have completed the activities for all the inventors, students play "Invention Jeopardy." Divide the class into teams. Each team decides on one spokesperson who will stand when he or she knows the correct answer. Assign one person to be the host. He or she selects a card at random and says the name of the invention. The team whose spokesperson stands first gets the first chance to tell who the inventor was to score a point for his or her team. Play continues until all the cards have been "played."

- Host a class-size "Invention Convention" for imaginative minds waiting for an opportunity to express themselves. Students may work in small groups for this activity. For introductory ideas, they may visit the "Build It Yourself" site and click the Famous Inventors link to read about original student inventions on the World Wide Web. When they are ready to begin their own creations, they must first think of an idea for a novel invention and design a model of it on paper. Students may use the Invention guide page 30, to help organize their thoughts. Then they use miscellaneous "junk" to create a working model of their invention. (Like all inventors of the past, if their model doesn't work when they test it, send them "back to the drawing board"!) Once the students have a working model, issue them an imaginary patent number. Then they create a poster explaining the invention's name, use, and a description of how it works to advertise it at the convention. If desired, have the students write a business letter to a prospective development company explaining why they should consider mass producing this idea. When all the students are ready, have an Invention Convention. Post students, creations, and posters around the room or media center. Invite parents and students from other classes to visit the convention to observe and ask questions of the inventors.

From the Imagination of

Name:_____

Directions: Think of an original invention. Consider its purpose and how it works. Write in complete sentences. Draw a diagram of it in the space below. Submit this form and a working model of your invention to your teacher who will issue you a patent number.

The name of my (our) invention is _____

It is necessary because _____

_____

_____

_____

The way it works is_____

_____

_____

_____

(For Official Use Only) Patent Number: _____

The Presidents

Objective:

Students will value this chance to research freely on the Internet as they investigate the presidents in U.S. history. They may follow the suggested Internet search instructions or use a search engine of their choosing to find appropriate sites from which to gather information.

Materials Needed:

- chalkboard or chart paper
- scrap paper
- writing paper
- small note cards
- one copy of page 33 for each team of students
- half sheet (8½ by 5½ inches) of plain white paper for each team
- colorful construction paper measuring 9 by 6 inches for each team
- large note cards
- drawing paper

Focus Web Site:

http://www.teachercreated.com/books/3804

Click on page 31, site 1

About This Site: This user-friendly presidential resource Web site is full of interesting facts and trivia about every president in U.S. history. Students click on the president of their choosing and then select from one of the many category links to learn more about specific areas of the presidents' lives. Included, also, are highlighted Internet links to additional sites and Web pages for those who wish to "dig deeper."

Alternative Web Sites:

http://www.teachercreated.com/books/3804

Click on page 31, sites 2, 3

Keywords for Search Engines:

Using your favorite search engine (such as **Google.com**) type keywords "U.S. Presidents" or the names of individual presidents.

Pre-Internet Activity:

Have the students brainstorm a list of personality traits they feel must be present in someone seeking the presidency. Write the traits they mention on the chalkboard or on chart paper. After the students feel the list is fairly complete, have them consider whether the current president possesses all of those traits. Discuss both positive and questionable actions the current president has taken which cause the students to assign or deny him the traits listed on the board. Have the students work in teams of three or four to decide on the five most important traits a president must have. They write them down on a small sheet of scrap paper. Gather the class together and tally the results. Circle the five traits with the most votes. The students then consider whether they could be president based on the list of the five most important qualities of a president.

Teaching the Lesson:

1. Allow the students to work in teams of two or three. List each president and his term(s) in office on a small note card. Have the students randomly select a president to research by choosing from the stack of cards.

2. Distribute a copy of page 33 to each team. They search the Internet using the URL and directions on the page or opt to try their luck with a reliable search engine of their choice. Students may use more traditional research materials if their Internet search does not supply them with the answers to all the questions on the research guide.

3. Once their research is complete, students draw a pencil drawing of their president on a half sheet of plain copy paper (8½ by 5½ inches) and then mount it onto a sheet of colorful construction paper measuring 9 by 6 inches. On a plain large note card they write the president's name in bold letters with a colored marker and write underneath his name brief facts they would like to share with a pen.

4. Have the students each consider their president's greatest accomplishment while he was in office. Have them design and create on a sheet of drawing paper a certificate of achievement for their president.

5. Post the students' artwork, fact cards, and certificates in the hall for others to appreciate.

6. (Optional) Have the students use their research guides to write summary reports of their presidents in a word processing program. Combine all the students' pages to make one book entitled "Presidential Publication."

The Presidents and Their Terms in Office					
George Washington	1776–1797	Abraham Lincoln	1861–1865	Herbert Hoover	1929–1933
John Adams	1797–1801	Andrew Johnson	1865–1869	Franklin D. Roosevelt	1933–1945
Thomas Jefferson	1801–1809	Ulysses S. Grant	1869–1877	Harry S. Truman	1945–1953
James Madison	1809–1817	Rutherford B Hayes	1877–1881	Dwight D. Eisenhower	1953–1961
James Monroe	1817–1825	James A. Garfield	1881	John F. Kennedy	1961–1963
John Q. Adams	1825–1829	Chester A. Arthur	1881–1885	Lyndon B. Johnson	1963–1969
Andrew Jackson	1829–1837	Grover Cleveland	1885–1889	Richard M. Nixon	1969–1974
Martin Van Buren	1837–1841	Benjamin Harrison	1889–1893	Gerald R. Ford	1974–1977
William H. Harrison	1841	Grover Cleveland	1893–1897	James E. Carter	1977–1981
John Tyler	1841–1845	William McKinley	1897–1901	Ronald W. Reagan	1981–1989
James K. Polk	1845–1849	Theodore Roosevelt	1901–1909	George H. W. Bush	1989–1993
Zachary Taylor	1849–1850	William H. Taft	1909–1913	William J. B. Clinton	1993–2001
Millard Fillmore	1850–1853	Woodrow Wilson	1913–1921	George Walker Bush	2001–
Franklin Pierce	1853–1857	Warren G. Harding	1921–1923		
James Buchanan	1857–1861	Calvin Coolidge	1923–1929		

Presidential Research Guide

Name _____

Directions: Go online to find out information about the president you selected. Fill in the blanks below with the facts that you learned.

1. Full Name of President_____

2. Date born to date died _____

3. Wife's name _____

4. Children's names _____

5. Educational background_____

6. Career before presidency_____

7. Party_____

8. Running mate_____

9. Election opponent(s) _____

10. Campaign slogan _____

11. Number of terms in office and dates _____

12. How he took office _____

13. Accomplishments while in office _____

_____

_____

14. Personal history _____

_____

_____

15. Other interesting information _____

_____

⚜ ⚜ ⚜ ⚜The Presidents (cont.)⚜ ⚜ ⚜ ⚜

Extended Activities:

- Have the students revisit the Internet Web site from which they gathered their information. They read carefully for little-known facts about their president and then write three simple trivia statements each on small note cards with the name of their president. Play "Presidential Trivia" one day during social studies. Divide the class into teams. Each team designates a spokesperson. Assign one student to read the trivia cards. When the teams think they know the answer, the spokesperson stands up. The reader calls on the first person to stand. If the spokesperson answers correctly, he/she wins one point for the team. If he/she answers incorrectly, the second person to stand has a chance to answer, and so on. Continue play until all the cards have been read. Place the cards at a learning center for students to study during their free time.

  Can students discover the answers to the following presidential trivia questions?

    › Who was the first American-born president? M. Van Buren
    › Which two presidents died on the same day? What was the date? J. Adams & T. Jefferson; July 4, 1826
    › Who was the shortest president? J. Madison (5' 4")
    › Which president held office for the shortest amount of time? W. Harrison (one month)
    › Which president was the first to get married in the White House? G. Cleveland
    › Which president had a pet cow? H. Taft
    › Which President gave the longest inaugural speech? W. Harrison (That's how he caught pneumonia and died so shortly after taking office.)

- Review some current "hot topics" the students are concerned about. Discuss the topic of campaign promises and how people running for the presidency address the issues that concern both themselves and the public the most. As president, the students may have a chance to correct a social wrong they consider needs attention. Have the students write an essay entitled "If I Were President . . ." They identify a current problem or situation they would like to see resolved and then explain possible ways they would go about correcting it if they were president. With parental permission, submit the students' writings to a local newspaper for publication.

- Review some campaign slogans the students discovered as they conducted their presidential research. Have them use what they know about their president to create an original campaign slogan for him. They design and create a campaign poster with their slogan as if that person were running for office today. Post them around the building for others to view. Students may also make campaign buttons if a button-making machine is available for this task. Encourage the students to wear their buttons each day during a unit about the presidents.

Native Americans

Objective:

The following pages feature activities related to four "tribes" scattered across the United States: the Iroquois, Pueblos, Seminoles, and Sioux. Students access Web sites and gather information about these four tribes. Then they summarize their findings in an individual booklet.

Materials Needed:

- United States map
- 1 copy of pages 38, 39, 40, and 41 for each student
- two sheets of plain white copy paper per student

Focus Web sites:

http://www.teachercreated.com/books/3804

Click on page 35, sites 1, 2, 3, 4

Alternative Web sites:

http://www.teachercreated.com/books/3804

Click on page 35, sites 5, 6

Keywords for Search Engines:

Using your favorite search engine (such as **Google.com**), type keywords "Iroquois," "Pueblo," "Seminole," or "Sioux." You can also try entering the tribe name with the word "tribe" after it for more specific results.

Author's Note: These Internet activities are designed to supplement a unit on Native Americans. Listed are just four of the many nations from across the United States that the class may study. Schedule one Internet visit per day if students will visit two or more of a nation's sites. These sites are quite expansive, and after the students complete the activity pages, they may wish to spend additional time exploring the sites for their own enjoyment.

Pre-Internet Activity:

On a United States map, show the students where the following states are located: South Dakota, Arizona, Florida, and New York. Have teams research common crops and climates of these four states and report their findings to the class. Ask the students how they think Native American tribes in these areas might have differed or been the same. Then complete the following activities for each of the tribes and compare the information at the end of the Internet lessons.

Teaching the Lesson:

1. Decide whether the students will access all the Native American sites spotlighted in these activities or just one or two. Most of the activity pages require students to link to related pages to find information and then click back to the home page to click a new link. For this reason, be sure to visit the suggested Web sites as a class.

2. Distribute the student activity page for the focus nation to each student. Review the United States map showing where many tribes of this nation live (see list below). Launch the destination URL, follow the directions, and answer the questions.

Iroquois–New York	Pueblos–Arizona
Seminoles–Florida	Sioux–South Dakota

3. If time permits, allow students time to explore links not mentioned on the activity page. Have them work in groups of three or four to record any interesting information they wish to share with the class.

4. After logging off, review what the students have learned. Have them make a four-page flip book describing the Nation (directions follow).

To make a four-page flip book:

- Fold one sheet of paper 2 ½" (6 cm) from the top.

- Fold a second sheet of paper 4 ½" (11.5 cm) from the top.

- Place the second folded sheet inside the fold of the first.

- Staple in place.

- Write a title on the top page.

- Write a detailed sentence at the bottom of each of the three remaining pages.

- Draw pictures to illustrate the text.

Native Americans (cont.) 🪨 🪨 🪨

Extended Activities:

Iroquois

Post a state map of New York. Visit the Web site listed on page 35 with the class. Assign six students, one for each reservation, the task of listening for the name of the city where each reservation is located. Mark these locations on the map by taping colorful construction paper circles measuring about 1" (2.5 cm) in diameter near where the reservations are located.

Have students use traditional means to learn more about the Iroquois longhouse. Have teams of students use brown construction paper to make a model of this dwelling. Place the students' models on a sheet of green poster board to create a replica of an Iroquois village. Then include probable land formations (rocks, trees, a river, etc.).

Pueblos

Write the names of the nineteen Pueblos on 6" x 9" (15 cm x 23 cm) inch note cards. Place them at a center for students to organize alphabetically. For younger students, only include five to ten tribes that begin with different letters.

Assign groups of two to three students the task of linking to a Pueblo of their choice, gathering information from the link, and then sharing a brief report of their findings with the class. Make a chart to compare the Pueblos. After all the groups have contributed, have the class remark on any similarities or differences that they observe among the Pueblos.

Pueblo Name	Fast Facts

Seminoles

Many Native American tribes have legends to explain events in nature. Students may read one such legend from the Seminoles at the site below. After reading one such legend, students can create an original legend of their own about an animal that is indigenous to their area.

http://www.teachercreated.com/books/3804

Click on page 37, site 1

Sioux

With the class, learn about the landmarks and legends of the Sioux. Have the students choose a landmark and, using the information they learn there, write an original legend about it.

With the class, learn about artifacts. The Sioux included drawings of their dreams on teepees as well as descriptions of traditional dress. Have the students cut a flattened brown paper bag into the shape of a teepee. Then they decorate it with drawings of dreams they would include if they were the dwellers in the teepee.

The Iroquois

The Onondaga Nation

1. What does the name "Onondaga" mean?

   _____

2. How would a member of the Onondaga tribe wear the feathers on his Gustoweh (feathered hat) to show that he is a member of that tribe?

   _____

   _____

The Oneida Nation

The people of the Oneida tribe have many stories and legends that teach about values and moral character. "The Legend of the Hermit Thrush" is one of these stories. Read the story and then answer the questions below.

3. How does the hermit thrush show that he is ashamed?

   _____

   _____

4. What happens when the hermit thrush sings his song?

   _____

   _____

5. Do you think it was worth it for the hermit thrush to learn his beautiful song? Why or why not?

   _____

   _____

   _____

   _____

The Seneca Nation

6. Which "door" do Senecas keep?

   _____

7. Who are the six nations of the Iroquois Confederacy?

   _____

   _____

Pueblos of the Southwest

Name:_____

Directions: After learning about the Pueblos of the Southwest, fill in the blanks below with the facts that you learned.

1. Circle the craft at which the Pueblos are very good.

   Pottery   Puzzles   Weaving   Jewelry   Leather work

2. Write three clans the Pueblos are divided into. _____
   _____

3. Besides English, write one other language Pueblos speak. _____

4. List three things you should do and three things you should not do when visiting a Pueblo.

   You should   **You should not**

   _____   _____

   _____   _____

   _____   _____

5. Read about one of the nineteen Pueblos. Write the name of the Pueblo and two interesting facts you learned about this community.

   _____

   _____

   _____

   _____

   _____

   _____

   _____

   _____

   _____

Seminoles

Name:_____

Directions: Read about the culture of the Seminoles.   Use the words from the word bank to fill in the blanks below.

chickee	sweetgrass	Muscogee
Sewing machine	Turban	Miccosukee

These are two languages still spoken by Seminoles today._____ _____

Baskets are made from _____.

A well-dressed Seminole man wears this on his head. _____

This word means "house." _____

This invention changed clothing styles beginning in 1900. _____

_____

Circle five of the eight clans from the Seminole Tribe.

Otter	Horse	Bear	Snake
Porcupine	Scorpion	Wind	Deer

The Great Sioux Nation

Name:_____

Directions: After learning about the Sioux Nation, complete the information below.

Overview

1. Write the names of two famous Sioux leaders. _____

_____

2. What does "Sioux" mean? _____

1800 1803 1806 1868 1874 1876

Milestones

3. In what year did Congress split the Great Sioux Nation into six smaller nations?

_____

Powwows

4. What does "wacipi" mean?_____

5. What kind of traditional food might you eat at a powwow?

_____

_____

_____

Mathematicians

Teacher Notes

NCTM Standards, Grades 5–8: Communication, Connections, and Number Relationships.

Objectives:

Students will…

- use the Internet to make an in-depth study of the biographies of three mathematicians.

- use the Internet to find out which mathematicians have the same birthday as they do.

Materials Needed:

- Computer with Internet access

- Poster board

Web Sites:

http://www.teachercreated.com/books/3804

Click on page 42, sites 1, 2, 3

Keywords for Search Engines:

Using your favorite search engine (such as **Google.com**), use keywords "famous mathematicians" and "mathematician birthday"

Time: approximately 2 hours

Teaching the Lesson:

- This lesson can be integrated with applicable social studies lessons.

- There are numerous Web pages about the history and people of mathematics. The student activity sheets list several good "jumping off" points for students to begin searching.

- In-depth biographies can be found on some of the specialized Web pages instead of the broad historical pages.

- For the regional research and biography sections, let students work in pairs or small groups.

Mathematicians (cont.)

Famous Mathematicians

Directions: Using Web sites as guides, select three famous mathematicians. For each mathematician you select, write a short, one-paragraph biography that includes information about their lives and their important contributions to mathematics. Select mathematicians from as many different backgrounds as you can.

1. Name of mathematician: _____

   Biography: _____

   _____

   _____

   _____

   _____

   _____

   _____

   _____

   _____

   _____

   _____

   _____

   _____

   _____

   _____

   _____

2. Name of mathematician: _____

   Biography: _____

   _____

   _____

   _____

   _____

   _____

   _____

   _____

   _____

3. Name of mathematician: _____

   Biography: _____

   _____

   _____

   _____

   _____

   _____

   _____

   _____

   _____

Mathematicians *(cont.)*

Name:_____

A Mathematician's Birthday

1. Go online and find a mathematician who was born in the same month as you.

Mathematician's name: _____ Date of birth: _____

2. Describe his or her major contribution to the field of mathematics:_____

   _____

   _____

3. If he or she were still alive, how old would he or she be? _____

   _____

   _____

Design a Birthday Card

In the space below, design a birthday card for your mathematician.

The Vikings

Objective:

Who pirated, marauded, stole, and still managed to find time to explore the Americas? Why, the Vikings, of course! Students get a glimpse into the life of these feared seamen as they learn about the history of the Vikings and some Viking lore. Then the students try their own play on words; instead of "going a-viking," will students "go a-literaring"?

Materials Needed:

- world map or globe
- one copy of page 48 for each student
- writing paper

Focus Web Site:

http://www.teachercreated.com/books/3804

Click on page 46, site 1

Alternative Web Sites:

http://www.teachercreated.com/books/3804

Click on page 46, sites 2, 3

Keywords for Search Engines:

Using your favorite search engine (such as **Google.com**), use keywords "Viking ship," "Viking everyday life," and "Viking Runes."

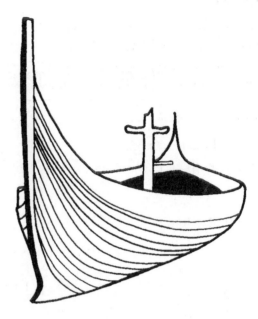

Pre-Internet Activity:

Explain to the students that long before Columbus made his historic voyage to the Americas, the Vikings had already been here and left, although they were known to have explored areas much farther north from where Columbus sailed. Originally, the Vikings set out from Scandinavia (Norway, Denmark, and Sweden) to conquer lands such as France, England, and northern Russia, to name a few. Some settled in Iceland; Eric the Red settled a colony in Greenland. They sailed all over and were known for their fierce bravery and uncompromising attacks. Show students the locations of the countries from which they sailed on a world map or globe. Then follow water routes to show the countries to which they traveled in search of riches. Explain to the students that they will have a chance to learn more about the Vikings on the Internet.

Teaching the Lesson:

1. The Vikings were known for their ruthless pursuit of wealth; they would do anything to get it and have no second thoughts about killing those who stood in their way. Explain that the Vikings are said to have been *pagans* or *heathens* because of their totally remorseless behaviors. Later Vikings began "practicing" Christian faiths, but their behaviors didn't change in the slightest.

2. Distribute a copy of page 48 to each student. Assist the students in logging onto the Internet, reading the information and answering the questions.

3. Explain that the terms *Vikings* and *Norsemen* tend to be used interchangeably. Norsemen were the people who lived in Scandinavia. The Norsemen who raided and pillaged were called Vikings (*Vik* meaning "harbor" or "bay"). When they went out on raids, they were said to be "going a-viking." Have the class work in small groups to come up with a term to use to describe events that occur during the school day.

   Example: reading might become "going a-literaring" or "going a-booking"

   Other possible daily activities:

lunch	grammar	erasing the board
recess	computers	sharpening pencils
math	snack	coloring
science	cleaning up	turning in work
social studies	listening	dismissal

✒ ✒ ✒ The Victorious Vikings ✒ ✒ ✒

Name:_____

Directions: Enter the Viking world. Use the information you find to answer the questions.

1. Draw a picture of a Viking Ship here:

2. List two interesting facts about Viking ships.

   - _____
   - _____

3. List two interesting facts about Viking everyday life.

   - _____
   - _____

The Vikings' written language used symbols called *runes*. Go online to find out how to write your name in runes. Write it in the box below.

✍ ✍ ✍ ✍ Web Tour Guides ✍ ✍ ✍ ✍

Opening Comments

Enthusiastic about Internet access at your school? Spread it around! That is one objective of this activity. It is also a great oral language exercise, and will give your students some solid practice at navigating through the web. But there is more! The audience gets worthwhile and focused exposure to the Net, and the activity also offers positive strokes for both presenters and presentees. Finally, it is never too early to size up your future students for, as you well know, it will not be long before these younger students are in your classroom.

Helpful Internet Site(s)

http://www.teachercreated.com/books/3804

Click on page 49, sites 1, 2, 3, 4, 5

Setting the Stage

- Pair your students ahead of time. (One older student and one younger student.) The older student should be the guide and the younger student should be the tourist. Have the guides interview the tourists, covering topics such as hobbies, after-school activities, places they have visited, favorite games, foods, and books.

- Armed with the interview data, brainstorm sites or subjects that would be interesting to these younger students.

- Let the guides browse to find other interesting, graphically oriented, or interactive sites.

- Hotlist these sites prior to the tour. Set up one large folder for the project or a separate folder for each guide.

Procedure

1. Match up less experienced tourists with experienced tour guides. It can be awkward for the guide if a younger student ends up navigating.

2. The guides should be willing to let the younger students control the mouse for part of the tour.

3. Make a list of all the sites your guides choose. You may not want them all hotlisted, but a text file can still be a great reference. Keep it open when you are browsing the Web and copy and paste the URLs into the location indicator for easy traveling in future sessions.

4. If there is time, let your guides rehearse.

5. Limit the tour to 10–15 minutes.

6. Video the tour sessions. Most students love to see themselves on TV, and guides who have not yet presented can learn a lot from those who have.

🌐 🌐 🌐 Web Tour Guides *(cont.)* 🌐 🌐 🌐

Name of tour guide:_____

Name of tourist:_____

Tour guides:

- Make sure you tell your travelers that they are here to see the World Wide Web.
- If they ask why it is called a web, tell them it is called a web because a lot of different places are connected, just like parts of a spider web. (You may want to sketch a spider's web to help explain the concept.)
- Tell the travelers you will take them to some places that you think they might like to see. Then, you will ask them where they would like to go.

The Tour Itinerary

Site #1:_____

One piece of information I want to share from this site:

_____

_____

Site #2: _____

One piece of information I want to share from this site:

_____

_____

Site #3: _____

One piece of information I want to share from this site:

_____

_____

Site #4 : (Tourist's Choice)   _____

_____

_____

Notes on my performance:

What went well: _____

_____

What I would do the next time:_____

_____

Language Arts

Individuals

Betsy Ross

Alexander Graham Bell

George Washington Carver

The Wright Brothers

Susan B. Anthony

Martin Luther King, Jr.

Jackie Robinson

Amelia Earhart

Charles Lindbergh

Explorers of the West

Betsy Ross

Objective:

What a Grand Old Flag! Students will enjoy learning about the history of "Old Glory" by referring to information about Betsy Ross on the Internet.

Materials Needed:

- 9" x 12" (23 cm x 30 cm) sheet of drawing paper for each student
- 1 copy of page 55 for each student
- 1 sheet of plain copy paper measuring 8 ½" x 11" (22 cm x 28 cm)

Focus Web site:

http://www.teachercreated.com/books/3804

Click on page 52, site 1

About this site: Simple organization with bountiful information about Betsy Ross and the history of the United States flag are all here at this Web site. Read the home page to learn general facts and answers to frequently asked questions. The links provide more in-depth insights while remaining simple enough to keep primary students' attention.

Alternative Web sites:

http://www.teachercreated.com/books/3804

Click on page 52, sites 2, 3, 4

Keywords for Search Engines:

Using your favorite search engine (such as **Google.com**), use keywords "Betsy Ross" and "United States Flag" or "American Flag."

Pre-Internet Activity:

Ask the students to draw and color the United States flag on a 9" x 12" (23 cm x 30 cm) sheet of drawing paper. (Hide the flag in the classroom first so they can't peek!) On the back, have them write three things they know about the flag. Then group the students into teams of three or four to share their representations and knowledge. As a class, discuss what differences, if any, the students observed about each other's drawings and information.

Teaching the Lesson:

1. Distribute a copy of page 55 to each student. Review it together to prepare for the investigation. As a class, launch the destination URL to access the "Betsy Ross Home Page." Complete questions one and two by reading the information here. Discuss how the students may link to related sites to retrieve the additional information necessary to complete the worksheet as well as arrow back to connect to another link.

2. Divide the class into teams of three or four. Allow the groups time to investigate this Web site as they search for the remaining answers to the questions.

3. George Washington preferred a six-pointed star; he thought they were easier to make. But Betsy showed him differently. Reconvene as a class to make the five-pointed star. Each student will need scissors and a plain white sheet of paper measuring 8 ½" x 11" (22 cm x 28 cm). You may access this information by launching the URL to the **Betsy Ross Home Page** and clicking the step-by-step directions to cut a 5-pointed star in one snip, or jump right to this page by launching it:

   http://www.teachercreated.com/books/3804

   Click on page 53, site 1

   Follow the directions on the page to make a star.

4. Have the students write one fact about the flag on their stars. Post on a bulletin board entitled "About Old Glory." Challenge the class to fill the board with 50 factual stars to represent the 50 states.

Betsy Ross *(cont.)*

Extended Activities:

- Have the groups explore additional links and write three interesting facts about Betsy Ross or the flag. The groups then use this information to write three trivia questions, each on the top of a folded sheet of 6" x 9" (15 cm x 23 cm) red, white, and blue construction paper. Have them cut out three additional stars, following the pattern from step 3 on page 53, to glue inside the folded paper. They write the answers on the star. Post the questions in the hallway or place them at a center for students to read independently.

- According to the information at this Web site, the first American flag disappeared without a trace. Pair up the students to write a possible legend to explain its mysterious disappearance. Students may create a completely unrealistic portrayal or use their knowledge of the history of the United States and colonial times to write a semi-realistic account. Combine the students' stories to make one book.

- As a class, brainstorm a list of details about the classroom. Discuss which items the students consider important enough to incorporate into a flag designed to represent their classroom. Give each student a 9" x 12" (23 cm x 30 cm) sheet of drawing paper to design and create a flag for the class. String the flags on a clothesline suspended from the ceiling.

- Have students research the history behind other countries' flags. They draw and color the nation's flag on a 6" x 9" (15 cm x 23 cm) sheet of drawing paper and give a brief report describing how it came to be in existence.

Betsy Ross and the Flag

Name:_____

Directions: Go online to learn about the American flag. Then use what you learned to fill in the blanks below.

1. List three feelings people experience when they view the American flag.

    _____   _____   _____

2. What do the colors of the American flag represent?

    Red stands for _____

    White stands for _____

    Blue stands for _____

3. Why would anyone fly a flag upside down?

    _____

4. Where did Francis Scott Key write the words to "The Star Spangled Banner"?

    _____

5. Which foreign country was the first to fly the American flag?

    _____

6. In what year did the flag have 30 stars? _____

    Which state does the thirtieth star represent? _____

Alexander Graham Bell

Objective:

Technology is quickly changing the communications field. Bring the students back to when it all began with Alexander Graham Bell in his laboratories conducting innumerable sound experiments. Students learn the "inner" workings of the human ear and play the role of Bell himself by conducting simple sound experiments.

Materials Needed:

- model of the human ear
- wire coat hangers
- string
- one copy of page 58 for each student
- writing paper
- styrofoam cups (one per student)
- yarn

Focus Web Site:

http://www.teachercreated.com/books/3804

Click on page 56, site 1

Alternative Web Sites:

http://www.teachercreated.com/books/3804

Click on page 56, sites 2, 3, 4

Keywords for Search Engines:

Using your favorite search engine (such as **Google.com**), use keywords "Alexander Graham Bell" and "how the ear hears" (with quotation marks).

Alexander Graham Bell (cont.)

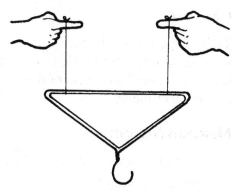

Pre-Internet Activity:

Display a model of the human ear. Discuss how sound travels (sound waves). Conduct this simple sound experiment to show that sound travels differently through various media. Attach yard-long lengths of string to the bottom corners of a wire coat hanger. Wrap the string around each index finger so the hanger is inverted. Tap the length of the hanger with a pencil. Have the students describe the sound. Then ask individual students to wrap the string around their index fingers and place them, gently, in their ears. Tap the hanger once again. Have the students who conduct the demonstration describe the sound to their classmates. Allow an opportunity for all students to experience the new sound. Tell the class that Alexander Graham Bell, whom we know as the inventor of the telephone, was fascinated with sound and vibrations and that they will have a chance to learn more about him on the Internet.

Teaching the Lesson:

1. Distribute a copy of page 58 to each student. Launch the destination URL with the class. Read the introductory paragraphs, and then allow teams of three to five students to follow the links to complete the activity page.

2. Review a model of the human ear. Have students volunteer to explain to the class how our ears change vibrations to intelligible sounds.

3. Have the students pretend they are Alexander Graham Bell conducting valuable sound experiments as part of their research. Have them write a summary of their observations.

   › Calculate the approximate time the sound of a bouncing ball takes to travel across different lengths of the playground.

   › Fill glasses or jars with varying amounts of water. Clink the glasses to produce different pitches of sound.

   › Have the students listen to sound through air by sitting upright and tapping desks with pencils, through water by tapping containers of water while putting their ears to the sides of the containers, and through solids by tapping their desks with pencils while their ears are resting on their desks.

   › Supply varying widths of rubber bands. Have the students pull them to varying degrees of tautness and "twang" them.

   › Have the students record everyday sounds with a tape recorder. They play their recordings for their classmates and have them guess what the sounds are.

🌰 🌰 🌰 Alexander Graham Bell 🌰 🌰 🌰

Name _____

Directions: Go online to learn about Bell as a teacher, tinkerer, and inventor. Read the information and answer the questions below.

1. Why do you think that Alexander Graham Bell was so interested in working with the deaf?

_____

_____

2. What was the name of Alexander Graham Bell's assistant?

_____

3. What were the first words Alexander Graham Bell spoke over the telephone?

_____

_____

Read about how the ear works. Number the order in which these events occur each time you hear a sound.

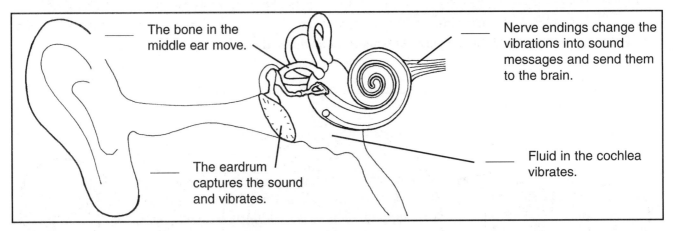

___ The bone in the middle ear move.

___ Nerve endings change the vibrations into sound messages and send them to the brain.

___ The eardrum captures the sound and vibrates.

___ Fluid in the cochlea vibrates.

Now you are going to do an experiment just like Alexander Graham Bell did! With a partner, make a "telephone" with yarn and two Styrofoam cups. Listen to each other across varying distances. Try making the yarn tight and then making it loose. Draw a picture below of how your telephone looked when you could hear each other the best.

Alexander Graham Bell (cont.)

Extended Activities:

- Use the study of Bell as an excuse to have the students practice their telephone manners. Review the words Bell first spoke to Watson over the phone ("Mr. Watson, come here, I want you!"). Discuss how Bell could have been more polite to his science partner. Have the students work in pairs to list three important tips for demonstrating good phone manners. Combine the students' thoughts onto one poster. Then discuss what to say if they are home alone, someone calls whom they don't know, they receive a "silent" caller, etc. Have the students practice phone manners with donated phones from home.

- Students can see an actual sound wave with this simple experiment. Attach a straight pin to the end of a tuning fork so the pin is extended off the end. After twanging the tuning fork, run the pin along a length of wax paper. The sound waves appear on the paper, similar to the way Bell's phonoautograph recorded sound with straw etching sound waves in glass.

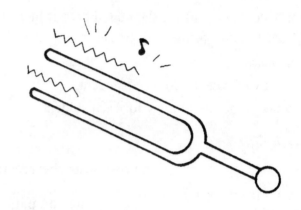

- Invite a local telephone worker to discuss with students how phone companies manage the extensive amount of phone line, how communications have changed over the past century, and the future of communications students have to look forward to.

George Washington Carver

Objective:

Inventions are not just contraptions that move and make noise. Students learn that many important discoveries were made by scientists such as George Washington Carver who worked with natural products to create useful synthetic products that are part of their everyday lives. They also decide what they consider his most important accomplishment and defend their views in a class debate.

Materials Needed:

- chalkboard
- empty containers listing the ingredients of bleach, mayonnaise, shampoo, and shaving cream
- construction paper for each student
- magazines
- one copy of page 62 for each student
- peanuts in the shell (a few for each student)

Focus Web Site:

http://www.teachercreated.com/books/3804

Click on page 60, site 1

Alternative Web Sites:

http://www.teachercreated.com/books/3804

Click on page 60, sites 2, 3, 4

Keywords for Search Engines:

Using your favorite search engine (such as **Google.com**), use keywords such as "George Washington Carver" and "chemurgy."

Pre-Internet Activity:

List these products on the chalkboard: bleach, mayonnaise, shampoo, shaving cream. Bring in an empty container of each common product. Distribute the containers to four students and have them read the ingredients in each product. List them under their headings on the board. Discuss how the students think these products were "invented." Explain that an African American named George Washington Carver was responsible for their production in the late 1800's to early 1900's and that more information about this inventor is awaiting them on the Internet.

Teaching the Lesson:

1. Discuss the difference between natural (from the earth) and synthetic (artificial or man-made) products. Explain that all of the items from the pre-Internet activity are synthetic since they aren't naturally occurring. Have the students cut out pictures from magazines to illustrate each topic; they glue natural products on the front and synthetic products on the back of a sheet of construction paper.

2. Before distributing peanuts to children for this activity, check for allergies.

3. Distribute a copy of page 62 to each student. If desired, launch the Web site as a class to complete question number one. Then allow the students to work in small groups to finish reading the information and completing the activity.

4. Review the products from the pre-Internet activity. How do they think these products have changed over the past 100 years or so?

5. Compile a class list of what the students consider to be Mr. Carver's most important discoveries. Have them defend their decisions in a class debate. Students form groups with classmates who agree with their own opinions as to Carver's single most important discovery. Then spokespersons from each group debate with one another in an attempt to persuade their classmates to agree with them.

Name:_____

Directions: Read the information about George Washington Carver. Answer the questions.

1. What is the definition of *Chermurgy*?_____

_____

2. George Washington Carver did most of his research with natural products. Can you name two of these products?

_____

_____

3. What do you think Mr. Carver's three most important inventions were?

_____

_____

_____

George Washington Carver is most remembered for his "invention" of peanut butter. Now, just like George Washington Carver, you can make your own product out of peanuts. Take apart the peanuts and observe them. What do you think you could make with them? It can be something edible or not edible. Draw an advertisement for your product in the box below.

The Wright Brothers

Orville and Wilbur Wright

Objective:

The Wright brothers are credited with producing and successfully flying the world's first "heavier-than-air" flying machine. Students learn the history of these two famous brothers and then demonstrate the physical factors Wilbur thought had ensured their success.

Materials Needed:

- writing paper
- drawing paper
- one copy of page 65 for each student
- nine-by-twelve-inch construction paper

Focus Web Site:

http://www.teachercreated.com/books/3804

Click on page 63, site 1

Alternative Web Sites:

http://www.teachercreated.com/books/3804

Click on page 63, sites 2, 3, 4, 5

Keywords for Search Engines:

Using your favorite search engine (such as **Google.com**), use keywords such as "Wright brothers" or "Wilbur and Orville Wright."

Teaching the Lesson:

1. Explain that the Wright brothers were determined to successfully fly a motor-driven aircraft when the world was saying it couldn't be done. They will learn more about this historic flight on the Internet.

2. Distribute a copy of page 65 to each student. Launch the Web sites with the class.

3. Allow the students time to work independently or in small groups to complete the activity page.

4. Have the students make a simple paper airplane with a nine-by-twelve-inch piece of construction paper. Use this three-dimensional figure to demonstrate the three axes of motion Wilbur considered when designing his aircraft (pitch, roll, and yaw). Explain that because of this consideration, he was really the only aircraft inventor at the time who would meet with success.

5. Have the students fly their paper airplanes. Then they redesign their model to try to make it fly farther and longer.

Extended Activity:

- Students who are very interested in learning more about this famous first flight can read the entire account as written by Orville Wright himself by visiting this site:

http://www.teachercreated.com/books/3804

Click on page 64, site 1

- This site offers the viewer a thorough graphic display of the Wright brothers and their involvement with the "flying machine."

http://www.teachercreated.com/books/3804

Click on page 64, site 2

🦅 🦅 🦅 A Famous First Flight 🦅 🦅 🦅

Name:_____

Directions: Read the information online and complete the activity with the facts you learned.

1. According to Wilbur Wright, what were the three elements of a flying machine?

_____

_____

2. Who was the pilot of the first flight? _____

3. How long did the first flight last? _____

In the columns below, list animals that can naturally fly, items that are extremely light and can "float" in the air or blow easily in the wind, and items that can fly without using a powered motor. The first one has been done for you.

animals that can fly	items that "float" in the air	items that fly without a powered motor
bird	paper	kite

In the boxes below, illustrate one item from each list. Show how it flies.

What do you think each of these things has in common with an airplane?

_____

_____

 # Susan B. Anthony

Objective:

People throughout the nation's history have struggled to achieve equality for all. Susan B. Anthony began her quest for equal voting rights for women in 1872 and worked toward her goal throughout her life. Her story is one of many successful achievements made by people willing to take a stand and fight for what they believed was just. Students experience her motivation firsthand as they learn about her life, her struggle, and her eventual success.

Materials Needed:

- one copy of page 68 for each student
- writing paper

Focus Web Site:

http://www.teachercreated.com/books/3804

Click on page 66, site 1

Alternative Web Sites:

http://www.teachercreated.com/books/3804

Click on page 66, sites 2, 3, 4

Keywords for Search Engines:

Using your favorite search engine (such as Google.com) use keywords such as "Susan B. Anthony" and "women equal rights."

Pre-Internet Activity:

Ask the students what they think might happen to them if they were to try to vote in the next election. Take a poll to see how many students would be interested in voting if they had the opportunity. Why can't they vote? Do they think the legal voting age of eighteen is fair? Why do they think eighteen is the age the lawmakers chose? Explain that women and minorities didn't used to have the right to vote. This was a privilege saved only for white, wealthy, male landowners. As times changed, though, Congress passed several amendments to the Constitution addressing the right to vote by all citizens. Susan B. Anthony led the suffrage movement, which eventually resulted in the passing of the nineteenth amendment. This ensured women the right to vote.

Teaching the Lesson:

1. Review the 14th and 15th amendments to the Constitution. The 14th outlawed slavery by guaranteeing citizenship to each person born in the United States. The 15th ensured that all men could vote regardless of race, color, or previous servitude. These two amendments prompted Susan B. Anthony to take action to obtain equal voting rights for women.

2. Distribute a copy of page 68 to each student. Launch the Web site as a class. Point out the first three links the students may access to learn about Susan B. Anthony. Follow the Online Tour link and read the "Welcome" page with the students. Continue to the Next link with the class, or allow students to work in small groups to tour her house and complete the student activity page.

3. The 19th amendment to the Constitution is sometimes referred to as the "Susan B. Anthony Amendment." Have students consider why her name should be associated with this amendment when it passed in 1920, fourteen years after her death. What must have occurred after her death? Why do they think this amendment took so long to pass? Have a small group of students further research the history behind Amendment 19.

Susan B. Anthony

Name:_____

Directions: Read about Susan B. Anthony online. Then complete the activity below.

Do you think that Susan B. Anthony was successful in her quest even though she died before women were given the right to vote? Explain your answer.

_____

_____

_____

Susan B. Anthony said that "Failure is impossible." Do you think that's true? Explain your answer.

_____

_____

_____

Can you think of a time when you achieved a goal by thinking that failure was impossible? Write a brief story about this time in the box below.

_____

_____

_____

_____

_____

_____

_____

_____

Martin Luther King, Jr.

Objective:

As leader of the Civil Rights era, Dr. King's involvement brought forth significant changes in the treatment of minority peoples. Students consider the unfair treatment minorities received and then create an "infowheel" of chronologically ordered events that took place in Dr. King's life.

Materials Needed:

- one copy of page 71 for each student
- one paper plate for each student
- one brad paper fastener for each student
- writing paper

Focus Web Site:

http://www.teachercreated.com/books/3804

Click on page 69, site 1

Alternative Web Sites:

http://www.teachercreated.com/books/3804

Click on page 69, sites 2, 3, 4

Keywords for Search Engines:

Using your favorite search engine (such as **Google.com**), use keywords "Martin Luther King, Jr."

Martin Luther King, Jr. (cont.)

Pre-Internet Activity:

Ask the students if they have ever felt as if they were not being treated fairly. Have them share their experiences. Ask them what they wished had happened differently which would have made them feel as if they were being treated fairly. Explain that not so long ago, African Americans in the United States were treated quite differently from everyone else; they could not attend the same schools, drink from the same fountains, eat where they pleased in restaurants, etc. Tell the students that Martin Luther King, Jr., was a peaceful leader in gaining equality for African Americans and other minorities and that they will learn about important events from his life on the Internet.

Teaching the Lesson:

1. Distribute a copy of page 71 to each student. They should cut and secure the "infowheel" to the plate before exploring the Internet. Students may write directly on their wheels as they gather information or select six date links and write the date and event on a separate sheet of paper before transferring it to their wheels.

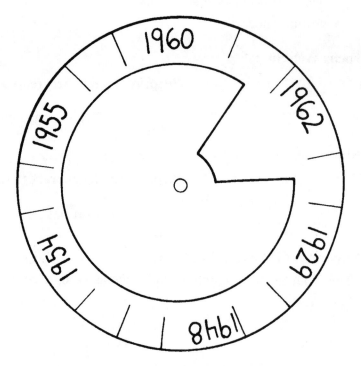

2. Allow small teams of students to access the Internet and gather the information. The dates on the wheels should follow in chronological order around the plates.

3. After everyone has completed the activity page, have each student choose a partner who was not in his or her Internet group. The partners share their infowheels with each other to learn more information about Dr. King from date links that they may not have accessed.

4. Following sharing time, have the students write a brief summary explaining what they learned about Dr. King.

Martin Luther King, Jr., Infowheel

Name:_____

Directions: Cut out the wheel below. Attach it to the center of a paper plate with a paper fastener. Use what you learned about Martin Luther King, Jr. to add the date of an important event to the outside edge of the paper plate. Write a description of the event in the space from the cutout section of the wheel. Illustrate the wheel.

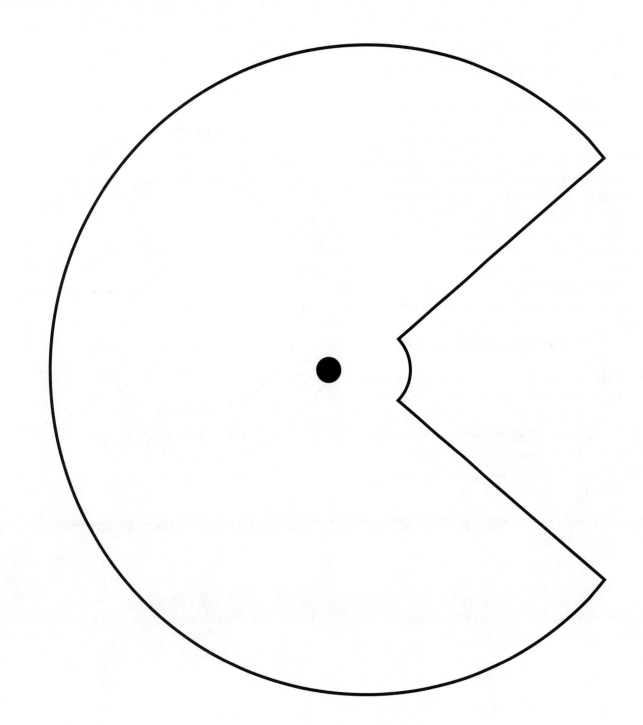

Extended Activities:

- Dr. King's most memorable speech was "I Have a Dream." Share this speech from a classroom resource book or by accessing either of the following Web sites.

http://www.teachercreated.com/books/3804

Click on page 72, sites 1, 2

Assign small groups of students a brief section of the speech to read and summarize. Students share the meaning of their portion with the class in order from the beginning of the speech to the end. Have students consider something they feel strongly about and write a two-to-three-minute speech on the topic of their choice. Have them practice their speaking skills by reciting their speeches to the class.

- Discuss injustices that are occurring around the world today by sharing some newspaper articles describing worldwide events. Have the students consider how Dr. King would react to these events. Students work in small groups to consider a dilemma of their choice. They list changes they think Dr. King would have liked to have seen occur and possible solutions to the problem.

- The Civil Rights movement was a time of unrest in our nation's history, even though Dr. King supported peaceful demonstrations. Have the students work in teams of three or four to use more traditional means to research an event from the Civil Rights era. Then they prepare a short skit of this action and perform it for their classmates.*

Civil Rights Era Notable Events

Brown v. Board of Education	March on Washington, D.C.
bus boycotts	Watts riot
sit-ins	Civil Rights Act of 1964
freedom rides	Voting Rights Act of 1965

---

*Author's Note: Use the second extended activity of "Jackie Robinson" on page 76 to complement the third extended activity above.

Jackie Robinson

Objective:

Students consider Jackie's difficult responsibility of being the first modern-day African American major league baseball player and compare his professional accomplishments to those of their favorite sports stars. Then they create true and false questions about Jackie and test their knowledge in a friendly game of "Jackie Robinson Grand Slam."

Materials Needed:

- chalkboard
- one copy of page 75 for each student
- writing paper
- five copies of the baseball bat pattern from page 74 for each pair of students

Focus Web Site:

http://www.teachercreated.com/books/3804

Click on page 73, site 1

Alternative Web Sites:

http://www.teachercreated.com/books/3804

Click on page 73, sites 2, 3, 4

Keywords for Search Engines:

Using your favorite search engine (such as **Google.com**), use keywords "Jackie Robinson."

Pre-Internet Activity

Have the students list some of their favorite professional sports heroes and tell why they admire them so much. List each celebrity under his or her appropriate sport heading on the chalkboard. Circle the names of those who are minority figures. Explain that some writers agree that without the efforts of Jackie Robinson, those people wouldn't have had an opportunity to play professional sports. Tell the students that they will have a chance to research on the Internet how Jackie Robinson paved the way for future minority players as well as aided the Civil Rights effort.

Teaching the Lesson:

1. Using the lists the students generated from the pre-Internet activity, discuss the contributions those athletes have made to their sports. How would sports be different if minorities were denied the right to play professionally?

2. The authors of the focus Web site deem Jackie Robinson as the "greatest athlete of the 20th century." What do the students think of this honor? Whom would they consider the greatest present-day athlete?

3. Distribute a copy of page 75 to each student. Students work as a class or in small groups to access the destination URL and complete the activity page.

4. After everyone has finished, have the students give the reasons why the authors consider Jackie Robinson to be the "greatest athlete of the 20th century." Have the students changed their minds regarding whom they would select since step 2?

5. Revisit the focus Web site as a class. Demonstrate how to write a true sentence from the information as well as change a factual statement into a false one. Give each pair of students five copies of the baseball bat pattern below. Allow the partners to access the focus Web site and write five true or false statements about Jackie Robinson. They write a "T" or "F" in the tip of the bat handle to indicate whether the sentence is true or false.

6. Use the facts and falsehoods to play "Jackie Robinson Grand Slam" either as a class or in small groups. The class or groups must first divide into two teams. One person is the caller. Each team member has a turn to state whether the sentence is true or false. After four correct answers, the team scores a "home run" and one point. The team loses its turn after three "strikes" or incorrect answers. Then the next team members take turns answering true or false. After all the statements have been posed, the teams tally their scores.

Big League Star

Name _____

Directions: Use what you learned about Jackie Robinson to complete this activity page.

1. Jackie's stardom was not easily achieved. List two hurdles he had to clear as he entered a world where no African American had been before. _____

   _____

2. Give an example of how Jackie's actions helped the Civil Rights movement. _____

   _____

3. Do you agree or disagree that Jackie Robinson was the "greatest athlete of the 20th century"? Why? _____

   _____

   _____

4. Think about one of your favorite sports figures. Compare Jackie Robinson's professional accomplishments to those of your favorite sports figure.

   _____

   _____

   _____

   _____

   _____

   _____

   _____

   _____

   _____

   _____

   _____

   _____

   _____

Jackie Robinson _(cont.)_

Extended Activities:

- Have the students use what they learned from the web sites for the activity to assign personality traits to Jackie. Was he humble? Aggressive? Timid? Have the students write a simple poem defining his character traits and the reasons for them.

- Jackie Robinson did his part to support the Civil Rights movement. As a class, access the link "An exclusive look at Jackie Robinson's involvement in the Civil Rights Movement." Discuss his involvement and the actions he took in the fight for equality for all. Have the class consider the advantages Jackie had over some other African American Civil Rights supporters that enabled him to encourage changes.

- Students may have an interest in discovering additional minority "barrier breakers" in other sports. Allow interested students to access the link "A look at African Americans who were barrier breakers in other sports." They research a sport of their choosing and write a report on paper cut and decorated to resemble a piece of athletic equipment from their respective sports. Post the students' work on a bulletin board entitled "The First Score."

- Have the students work in pairs to create a mock television interview between a news reporter and Jackie Robinson. Students may select any event from Jackie's life on which to base a dialog. They perform their skits for the class.

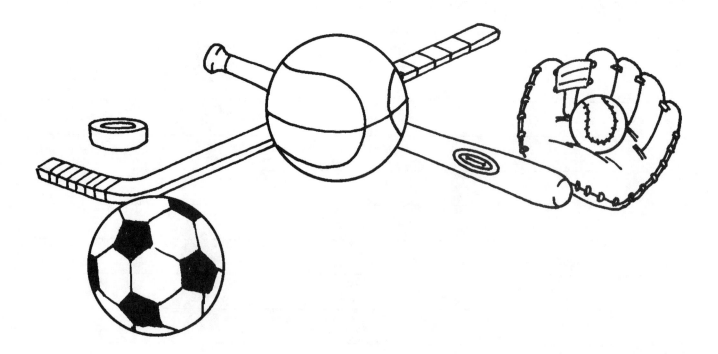

 # Amelia Earhart

Objective:

Students travel the world with Amelia Earhart, mapping out their own route and then comparing it to the one she flew as she attempted to circle the earth in an airplane. Students also learn and apply military time as it pertained to Earhart's disappearance.

Materials Needed:

- world map
- chalkboard
- one copy of page 79 for each student

Focus Web Site:

http://www.teachercreated.com/books/3804

        Click on page 77, site 1

Alternative Web Sites:

http://www.teachercreated.com/books/3804

        Click on page 77, sites 2, 3

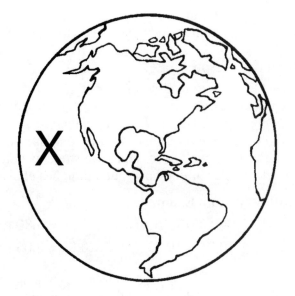

Keywords for Search Engines:

Using your favorite search engine (such as **Google.com**), use keywords "Amelia Earhart."

Amelia Earhart (cont.)

Pre-Internet Activity:

On a world map, have the students determine the shortest possible route if they were to travel around the world, beginning in their hometown, circling the globe, and returning to their hometown. (Explain that the students can travel only up to 2,000 miles at a time.) Would they travel east around the Earth or west? How long would they expect this journey to last? What would be some possible dangers in attempting this excursion? Explain that Amelia Earhart attempted to achieve this goal but disappeared over the Pacific Ocean while she was on the last leg of her journey. The students will read on the Internet more about her flight and the controversy her disappearance stirred.

Teaching the Lesson:

1. Lead a discussion about military time. (*Every time has two hour positions and two minute positions. Hours are counted similarly to civilian time from one second after midnight until 12 noon—12 hundred hours. Then the hours continue counting up until 12 midnight—24 hundred hours. To read afternoon civilian time, subtract 12 from the hour position.*) Write several military times on the chalkboard and have students determine the civilian time. Students should also practice determining how much time has elapsed between two military times.

   Military Time Examples:

04:56 = 4:56 A.M.	15:30 = 3:30 P.M.
10:25 = 10:25 A.M.	20:05 = 8:05 P.M.

2. Distribute a copy of page 79 to each student. As a class or working in small groups, have the students access the focus Web site and complete the activity page.

3. As a class, follow Earhart's flight stops around the world. Compare her pattern to those the students mapped out in the pre-Internet activity.

   1 Los Angeles, CA, to Miami, FL

   2 to San Juan, Puerto Rico

   3 to the northeast edge of South America

   4 to Africa

   5 to the Red Sea

   6 to Karachi, Pakistan

   7 to Rangoon, Burma

   8 to Bangkok, Thailand

   9 to Singapore, Malaysia

   10 to Port Darwin, Australia

   11 to Bandung, Indonesia

   12 to Lae, New Guinea

   13 toward the Howard Islands

Earhart's Final Flight

Name:_____

Directions: Read the information online and answer the questions about Amelia Earhart's final flight.

1. In which U.S. state did Amelia Earhart's final flight begin?

   _____

2. What was the date of the final flight?

   _____

3. What was the date of the last transmission?

   _____

4. Read the theories describing Earhart's disappearance. Do you believe any of them? Select one of the theories or think of one of your own. Use this theory to write a legend explaining Earhart's disappearance. Use the back of this page if you need more space.

   _____

   _____

   _____

   _____

   _____

   _____

   _____

   _____

   _____

   _____

   _____

   _____

   _____

Charles Lindbergh

Objective:

Students consider the motivation Lindbergh had for attempting to fly solo, nonstop over the Atlantic Ocean. Then they access the Internet to gather clues to discover his hometown.

Materials Needed:

- one copy of page 82 for each student
- U.S. map or U.S. desktop maps

Focus Web Site:

http://www.teachercreated.com/books/3804

Click on page 80, site 1

Alternative Web Sites:

http://www.teachercreated.com/books/3804

Click on page 80, sites 2, 3, 4

Keywords for Search Engines:

Using your favorite search engine (such as **Google.com**), use keywords "Charles Lindbergh."

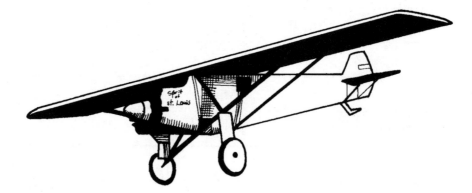

Pre-Internet Activity:

Lead a discussion about what motivates people to do things that have never been accomplished before. What would the students be willing to do for $25,000.00? Explain that Lindbergh attempted to be the first person to complete a solo, nonstop flight over the Atlantic Ocean when airplanes and aviation were still fairly new concepts. Have the class brainstorm the hazards and dangers that he might have faced and how he might have prepared for his flight. Then explain that he did it to win a $25,000.00 prize. Was this prize money worth the effort? Of course, his success brought more than prize money. Overnight (literally), Lindbergh became a famous hero. How does this label add to the glory of his accomplishment?

Teaching the Lesson:

1. Review with students how to write a newspaper article. Introduce the six question words that the article should answer: who, what, where, when, and why. Discuss with them the excitement that a newspaper reporter would have felt in 1927 when reporting on this historic event.

2. Allow students time to read the information available online about Charles Lindbergh. Have them think about what they want to write about in their newspaper articles.

3. (Optional) Help the students use the legend on a world map to measure the distance between New York and Paris. Divided by the $33\frac{1}{2}$ hours he took to complete his mission, the students will discover his average speed (mph). How does this velocity compare with modern flights? Invite a local travel agent to come to your class to share the time it takes to travel from one city to another across the Atlantic Ocean.

☙ ☙ ☙ ☙ ☙ ☙ "Lucky Lindy" ☙ ☙ ☙ ☙ ☙ ☙

Name:_____

Directions: Write a newspaper article about Charles Lindbergh's famous flight. Use the information you learned from the web sites you visited. Make sure that you answer the six question words: who, what, when, where, and why.

EXTRA!!! The Times EXTRA!!!

Touchdown in Paris!

_____

_____

_____

_____

_____

_____

_____

_____

_____

_____

_____

_____

_____

_____

_____

Explorers of the West

Objective:

Research a historical figure or the exploration of a geographic location.

Suggested Internet Sites:

http://www.teachercreated.com/books/3804

Click on page 83, sites 1, 2, 3, 4, 5

Setting the Stage:

- Have students choose a person or geographic area to study.
- Because it may be difficult to find information through the above resources, you may want to have your students also do Web searches by topic.
- Review the requirements for this assignment.
- Give a fixed time to explore some of the Web sites and their links.

Procedure:

- Students will research an explorer or area of exploration.
- Students will keep a record of Web sites visited and resources used.
- Students will present their information to the class or a chosen group.

Special Considerations:

- This would be a great project for a group to complete.
- Consider having groups present their information with oral reports to the class.

Explorers of the West *(cont.)*

Name:_____

Notes and Information

1. Choose a person or geographic area to study.
2. Visit Web sites to gather information.
3. Complete the form below and present your information to the class.

Name of explorer_____ Nationality _____

Born _____ Died _____

Geographic area(s) of exploration _____

Web sites used (URL) _____

_____

_____

Three things that I found interesting about this person:

1. _____

2. _____

3. _____

Three items of interest about this person's travels:

(Be sure to include problems with the trip as well as the parts that went well.)

1. _____

2. _____

3. _____

History

Immigration

The History of Aviation

The Olympics

Popcorn

The Ancient World

Immigration

Objective:

Since its birth as an English colony, people have been immigrating to the lands that make up the United States from all over the world. Students compare the differences immigrants of the 1600s faced versus immigrants of the 1800s and even those of today. They organize the information according to years and then write a journal entry for each era of immigration.

Materials Needed:

- chalkboard or chart
- drawing paper
- copies of page 88
- four large note cards for each group
- extra writing paper

Focus Web Site:

http://www.teachercreated.com/books/3804

Click on page 86, site 1

Alternative Web Sites:

http://www.teachercreated.com/books/3804

Click on page 86, sites 2, 3

Keywords for Search Engines:

Using your favorite search engine (such as **Google.com**), use keywords such as "immigration," "immigrants," or "Ellis island."

Immigration (cont.)

Pre-Internet Activity:

Have the students share their ancestral heritages (German, Greek, Russian, Cuban, etc.) and, if they know, the approximate year their ancestors first arrived in the United States. Write the ethnic groups the students mention on the chalkboard or on a chart. Assign each student or pair of students a different country for which to draw a flag so that as many countries' flags as possible are represented. Suspend them from the ceiling or post them in the hall with the heading "Arrived from Many Nations."

Teaching the Lesson:

1. Have the students think of reasons why people would want to leave their native countries and emmigrate to the United States. Then have them consider how immigrants arrived when our nation was first born and compare that to how they think immigrants of today arrive.

2. Have students consider the following while doing their research.

   ⇨ Reasons for immigration

   ⇨ Who were/are the immigrants to the U.S.?

   ⇨ Peaks/waves of immigrants

   ⇨ Methods of transportation and ports of arrival

   ⇨ Process of entering the U.S.

   ⇨ Destination/places where they settled

   ⇨ Treatment/reception by other Americans

   ⇨ Effects/impact on America (positive and negative)

   ⇨ Opportunities for and success of immigrants

   ⇨ Assimilation? If so, to what degree?

   ⇨ What did/do immigrants find distinctive about America?

   ⇨ Legal vs. illegal immigrants

   ⇨ Laws restricting immigration

3. Tell students that they are going to pretend to be an immigrant from a time period of their choosing. Have them complete page 88 as if they are being interviewed about their immigration experience.

4. (Optional) Have students write journal entries from an immigrant's perspective.

Immigration *(cont.)*

Name:_____

Directions: Pretend that you are an immigrant in the time period you have chosen. A historian would like to interview you about your immigration experience. Answer the questions below as honestly as you can.

Where did you emigrate from?

_____

In what decade did you arrive in the United States?

_____

How did you get here?

_____

_____

Where did you first live when you arrived here?

_____

_____

What kind of work did you do when you first arrived?

_____

_____

How did people treat you?

_____

_____

_____

Do you think that emigrating from your country was the right choice? Explain your answer.

_____

_____

_____

_____

Immigration *(cont.)*

Extended Activities:

- Ellis Island played an important role in the immigration process during our nation's history. These Web sites provide an inside look at this now historical site once filled with eager, yet apprehensive, newcomers to the United States.

http://www.teachercreated.com/books/3804

Click on page 89, sites 1, 2, 3, 4

Have the students experience Ellis Island firsthand by having "Coming to America" day. Prior to the big event, write new names on cards, one for each student. Assign an area in the classroom to be the "deportation area." Students must first submit a simple entry application including their names, country of origin, and reasons for wanting to immigrate to the United States. Line up the students outside the classroom door. They attempt to gain entry at Ellis Island (with you acting as the immigration official). When students first arrive, tape a new name to their clothes. Speaking in jibberish, assign them a place to stand in the room. You reserve the right to "deport" anyone who is acting up, argumentative, or suspicious looking. Once everyone has entered, begin immigration proceedings. First, they must pass the test. Begin in one area and ask obscure, ridiculous, or historical questions of each student. Students answering incorrectly must go to the deportation area. Finally comes the medical exam. Pretend to check the students' eyes, tongues, and ears. Anyone failing the medical exam must also go to the deportation area. After all the students have had their chance to pass through Ellis Island, discuss their emotions and concerns as well as the fairness of the proceedings. Relate these feelings to how real immigrants might have felt coming into Ellis Island.

- Value the ethnic diversity of the class by having a cultural feast. Each family supplies an ethnic dish to share with the class. Invite parents and relatives to share in the celebration as well. Provide ethnic games to play, if possible. Set a time and date, and let the celebration begin!

The History of Aviation

Objective:

Students consider the elements of flight and modern flying experiences before they learn about the pioneers of aviation (before and after the Wright brothers). Then they create a model of an early aircraft.

Materials Needed:

- writing paper
- one copy of page 92 for each student
- drawing paper or tagboard
- patterns on page 93
- thread

Focus Web Site:

http://www.teachercreated.com/books/3804

Click on page 90, site 1

Alternative Web Sites:

http://www.teachercreated.com/books/3804

Click on page 90, sites 2, 3, 4

Keywords for Search Engines:

Using your favorite search engine (such as **Google.com**), use keywords such as "flight history" and "aviation history."

The History of Aviation (cont.)

Pre-Internet Activity:

Take a walk outside. Have the students sit quietly and observe birds in flight. (Students may also make observations through the window.) They consider and jot down all the scientific factors that come into play when a bird flies through the air (e.g., wind speed and direction, gravity, wing span, weight of the bird, etc.). Place the students into groups of four or five to share their ideas with their classmates. As a class, students share ideas that everyone seems to have in common as well as a few unique individual ideas members of their group share. Explain that although we take airplanes and flight (aviation) for granted now, in the days when this was a new field, many people experimented with different aircraft in trial-and-error attempts to be the first to "fly."

Teaching the Lesson:

1. Have the students share any flying experiences they may have had: the foods they were served, using the facilities, the kind of seats, other surroundings, etc. Ask the class whether they think these surroundings are comfortable. Explain that the men who first attempted to fly did so usually standing up or suspended in air. No stewardesses came to take their lunch orders nor did they have handy airsick bags and bathrooms. Not that they needed them; the first flights lasted mere seconds. Tell the students that they will have a chance to learn about three men who were the earliest, but not always successful, pioneers in the field of aviation.

2. Distribute a copy of page 92 to each student. As a class or in small groups, access the Web sites and complete the activity page.

3. Airplanes improved dramatically and rapidly as the world entered the 20th century. Have the students use the recommended websites for this activity to select two different types of historical aircraft. They will list the name, country of origin, and history for each. They will also draw a picture of each aircraft.

4. Have students create models of one of the airplanes from the activity page. They can use drawing paper or heavy tagboard to cut and glue a model of a plane and color or paint its markings. (The patterns on page 93 may be helpful if the plane has a similar body style. If not, the students may use the patterns as guides to create their models.) They can share the planes and information with the class. Attach a length of thread to the tops of the planes and suspend them from the ceiling.

Extended Activity:

Invite an aviation expert from a local or international airport to come to your class and further discuss the history of aviation and how advances in this field affected American society.

The History of Aviation _(cont.)_

Name:_____

Directions: Select two airplanes from those listed on the websites. Answer the questions below and draw a picture of each plane.

Aircraft #1

What is the name of the aircraft? _____

What country was the aircraft from? _____

What is the history of the aircraft? _____

Draw a picture of the aircraft in the box below.

Aircraft #2

What is the name of the aircraft?_____

What country was the aircraft from? _____

What is the history of the aircraft? _____

Draw a picture of the aircraft in the box below.

The History of Aviation (cont.)

Use these patterns with step 4 from page 91.

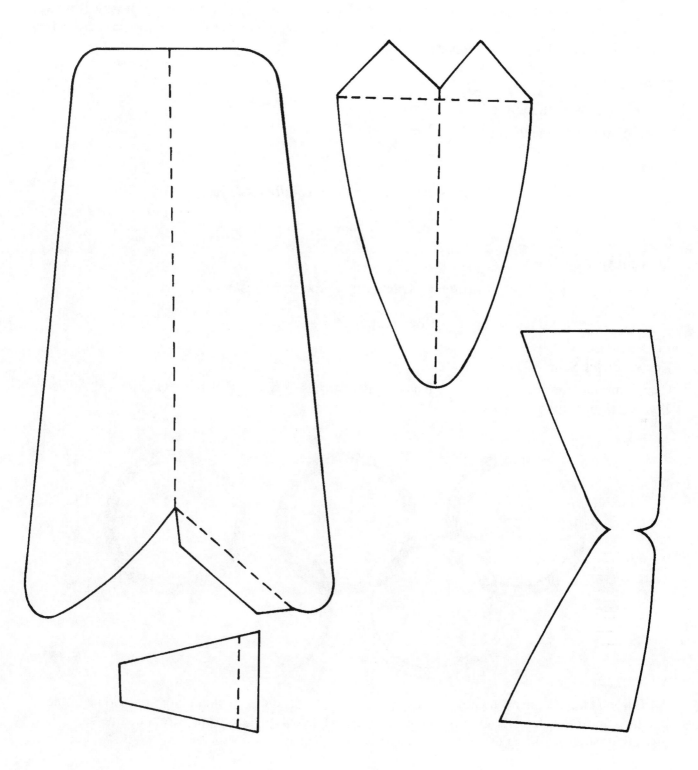

The Olympics

Objective:

Let the games begin! Students apply their math skills to calculate the number of years ago the first Olympics began as well as the number of years they lasted. They begin to consider differences between the ancient and modern games in the classroom and then go online to learn more differences as well as reading about actual ancient Olympians.

Materials Needed:

- calculators (optional)
- one copy of page 96 for each student

Focus Web Site:

http://www.teachercreated.com/books/3804

Click on page 94, site 1

Alternative Web Sites:

http://www.teachercreated.com/books/3804

Click on page 94, sites 2, 3

Keywords for Search Engines:

Using your favorite search engine (such as **Google.com**) use keywords such as "Olympics," "Ancient Olympics," or "Olympic Games."

Author's Note: The men who competed in the ancient games did so without clothing. Some of the graphics (mostly etchings, carvings, or cartoons) reveal the Olympians from a front or side view. Use discretion when accessing these sites with students.

The Olympics *(cont.)*

Pre-Internet Activity:

Lead a discussion about the students' favorite Olympic sports and competitors. Ask them to identify the location of the most recent Olympic games. Explain that the Olympics began in Greece in 776 B.C. Ask the students to recall the prizes the winners received. Explain that early victors were awarded head wreaths made of olive tree branches. The students then recall some sports of the modern Olympic games. Explain that the very first Olympics had only one running event but soon included numerous running events and other sports. Tell the students that they will have a chance to further investigate the differences between the ancient and modern Olympic games on the Internet as well as read about an actual ancient Olympian.

Teaching the Lesson:

1. Help the students discover how many years ago the first Olympics took place. Then they consider all the advancements and changes the world has witnessed throughout that time. Besides the above-mentioned comparisons, how else do the students think the ancient Olympics differed from the modern games?

2. Explain that the ancient Olympics ended around 394 A.D. Help the students discover the duration of the ancient Olympics. (*1,170 years*) Explain that in this amount of time, many changes took place in the games. They will compare this period of time known as the "ancient" Olympics to the "modern" games which date back to 1896, only a little over one hundred years ago.

3. Distribute a copy of page 96 to each student. If desired, launch the Web site as a class. Read the information there and have the students complete numbers 1, 2, and 3 on their sheets.

4. Divide the class into five groups and assign each team to research one of the five ancient Olympians, or have the students work with a partner to select an Olympian of their choice. Have the students share their research with the class.

Olympic Background Information

- The Greek calendar was based on the Olympiad (four-year interval between games).

- Hercules founded the games.

- Temples and statues were erected to honor Zeus.

- The games were canceled during WWI (1916) and WWII (1940 and 1944).

- In 1992, the winter and summer games began alternating every two years.

The Olympics *(cont.)*

Name:_____

Directions: The original Olympics were very different from the events the world celebrates in modern times. Read online about how the Ancient Olympics were different from the modern games. List three of these differences below.

Ancient Games   **Modern Games**

1. _____   _____

   _____   _____

2. _____   _____

   _____   _____

3. _____   _____

   _____   _____

Follow the links on the websites to learn about ancient Olympians. Select one and read his story. Then complete the information below.

His name _____

His sport _____

Year(s) he participated _____

How he became an Olympian _____

_____

_____

_____

_____

_____

_____

_____

Extended Activities:

- Have a small group of students apply their Internet research skills to discover where the next three Olympic games (summer and winter) will be held.

- Besides a little bit of history, students can learn about some Olympic ceremony protocol at the third alternative Web site listed on page 94. As a class, link to the Olympic Oath. Have a volunteer read the oath to the class. Discuss the purpose of this or any oath. What does it mean to take an oath? Who else takes an oath? (*doctors, witnesses, the President, etc.*) Have the students work with a partner to write a classroom oath. To what will they pledge their word? Post them all for the class to read and consider the words before starting each day.

- Have students learn more about the Olympic flag. Have them consider the Olympic motto and how it applies to athletes as well as everyday activities.

- Hold a mini-Olympics in your classroom. Have small groups of students work together to create an opening ceremony performance lasting between two and three minutes in length. Some ideas include jumping rope, juggling, dancing, flag waving, etc. Then assign each student a country to represent in the Olympic games. (Depending on the number of students, you may have as few as four or as many as eight countries. Each country should have five to eight representatives.) Each person must participate in a different event from his or her teammates. Following are some ideas for events and how winners are determined. Keep track of the first, second, and third place winners. Make gold, silver, and bronze medals from construction paper and attach them to a length of yarn for the students to place over their necks during the awards ceremonies following the games.

straw javelin (distance)	running long-jump (distance)
cotton ball shot put (distance)	string hurdles (time)
running races (time)	crab-walk soccer (score)
Frisbee™ discus (distance)	basketball shots (count)

Popcorn

Objective:

Students will burst with excitement when they learn the history of one of America's favorite snacks.

Materials Needed:

- chalkboard
- 1 copy of page 101 for each student
- research materials
- yarn
- note cards
- sentence strips

Focus Web site:

http://www.teachercreated.com/books/3804

Click on page 98, site 1

Alternative Web site:

http://www.teachercreated.com/books/3804

Click on page 98, site 2

Keywords for Search Engines:

Using your favorite search engine (such as **Google.com**), use keywords such as "popcorn" or "history of popcorn."

Popcorn (cont.)

Pre-Internet Activity:

Have the students share how their family pops popcorn. Write their responses on the board. Then ask the students if they know where popcorn originated. Most students may already know that Native Americans used corn well before explorers and settlers arrived. What they may not realize is that they enjoyed popped corn then as much as we enjoy it today. Ask the students how they think the Native Americans popped corn without the use of modern conveniences. Tell them that they will have an opportunity to discover the extraordinary Native American way to pop corn as well as learn interesting information about this snack, including popcorn's "seedy" history.

1. Distribute a copy of the student activity sheet on page 101 to each student. Review the directions, and then allow time for small groups of students to access the Internet to complete the activity.

2. Challenge students to use traditional means to learn more about the history of popcorn. Make a large wall-sized time line with a piece of yarn. Include the years from the student activity page on small blank note cards. Write the events on sentence strips and include them on the line. Add years and events to the time line as students make their discoveries. Who would have imagined popcorn has such a abundant history?

Extended Activities:

- Have students make a popcorn popping guide to place in the library using information that they have learned online. Assign groups of students to acquire one popcorn popping tip from each of the three categories, *Popping Tips, Storage Tips,* and *Saving "Old Maids."* (If groups write down the same tip, one of them will have to return to the computer to discover an additional tip.) Then the groups write and illustrate their tip on a sheet of drawing paper. Combine the pages to make a popcorn popping guide. Include a table of contents, title page, and cover. Bind the pages into a book and place it in the library for others to enjoy.

Popcorn *(cont.)*

- Now that the students have learned about the early and European histories of popcorn, you might find the information lends itself to a lesson on cause and effect. Randomly post the causes in one column and effects in another. Have small groups of students write two matching cause and effect sentences on paper.

Cause	Effect
Popcorn was a popular food.	Street vendors sold a lot of popcorn to crowds.
Popcorn was inexpensive.	Even poor families during the Great Depression could afford this luxury.
Sugar was sent overseas to help the troops during World War II.	There was no sugar to make candy, so Americans ate popcorn.
Television became more popular than going to the movies.	TV viewers began eating popcorn at home.
The microwave oven was invented.	Popcorn was the first food tested by the use of microwave heating.
Popcorn is a popular snack even today.	Americans eat about 68 quarts of popcorn each year.

- Find out more about the composition and nutritional value of popcorn. Students may practice their chart reading skills or create a pie chart to demonstrate the composition of popcorn.

- End the discovery of popcorn with a popcorn eating festival. Try topping this snack with a variety of different spices: salt, seasoned salt, chili powder, or cinnamon. Parmesan and powdered cheddar cheeses also make great toppings. What other original flavors are your students brave enough to try?

Popcorn in History

Name: _____

Directions: Learn about popcorn online. Then complete the timeline by cutting and pasting the correct answers in the spaces provided.spaces provided to show the year each event occurred.

1492   1519   1612   1621   1650   1600s–1700s

French explorers mention the making of popcorn soup by the Iroquois.

Colonists have their first taste of a "puffed" breakfast cereal-popcorn!

Cortes finds popcorn in Mexico.

Chief Massasoit shares popcorn with the Pilgrims at the first Thanksgiving feast.

Cobo writes about the use of popcorn by the Peruvian Indians.

Natives tried to sell popcorn to Columbus.

The Ancient World

Objective:

Give your students an overview of ancient civilizations, their location, everyday life and culture.

Materials Needed:

The Ancient World activity sheet

Web Sites:

http://www.teachercreated.com/books/3804

Click on page 102, sites 1, 2

Teaching the Lesson:

1. Introduce students to general information about the ancient world. (This can be found at **http://www.teachercreated.com/books/3804 Click on page 102, site 3.**)

2. Do a demonstration of the site with the entire class, or have the students fill in the activity sheet individually or in small groups of two to four students.

Alternative Web Site:

http://www.teachercreated.com/books/3804

Click on page 102, sites 4, 5

Keywords for Search Engines:

Using your favorite search engine (such as **Google.com**), use keywords such as "ancient civilizations," "Greek Mythology," "Roman Mythology," "Classical Archaeology," and "Mediterranean Archaeology."

The Ancient World

Name:_____

Identify and give the location of five civilizations that were prominent in the Ancient World:

1. _____

2. _____

3. _____

4. _____

5. _____

On the timeline shown below, mark and label the approximate duration of the civilization's prominence. **(Note:** We will only be charting through Medieval times). The time span will be from 3000 B.C. to approximately A.D. 1100.

/ _____ /

starting date   present date
3000 B.C.

The Seven Wonders

Help your students to identify the Seven Wonders of the Ancient World. Discuss their locations and their importance in the development of civilization.

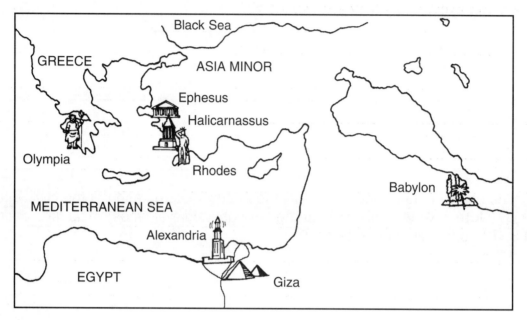

Materials Needed:

The Seven Wonders activity sheet

Web Site:

http://www.teachercreated.com/books/3804

Click on page 104, site 1

Teaching the Lesson:

1. Many of the achievements of ancient civilizations are known only through writings and pictures. Of the original Seven Wonders of the World, only one, the Great Sphinx, is still in existence. Ask students why they think these other wonders are no longer in existence.

2. Ask students why the ancient civilizations felt the need to make these large-scale monuments.

3. Ask students if they think civilization still has a need to create large-scale monuments. If so, have students give some examples of such monuments.

Extended Activities:

1. Ask students if there are any regions of the world where religion still promotes the building of large temples and other buildings. If so, have then give some examples.

2. Ask students what keywords they might use if they wanted to get additional information. Have them list several possible keywords related to the Seven Wonders of the Ancient World. Then have them do a search.

The Seven Wonders (cont.)

Name:_____

Using the information you learned from the Internet, identify the Seven Wonders of the Ancient World and explain why they are "wonderful."

1. _____

_____

2. _____

_____

3. _____

_____

4. _____

_____

5. _____

_____

6. _____

_____

7. _____

_____

List at least three modern-day achievements which might qualify as "wonders" of the modern world including explanations as to why you think they are worthy of being called "wonders."

_____

_____

_____

_____

_____

Discover the Ancient World

Objective:

Provide your students with a simple introduction to archaeology and cultures of the ancient world.

Materials Needed:

Investigating the Ancient World activity sheet

Learn About Ancient Architecture activity sheet

Web Site:

http://www.teachercreated.com/books/3804
Click on page 107, sites 1 and 2

Teaching the Lesson:

1. Archaeology is the scientific study of the cultures of peoples of the past. The purpose of archaeology is to understand how humans in the past interacted with their environment, and to preserve this history for present and future learning.

2. After reading the information from the "What is Archaeology?" site, students can do some exploration of their own into the world of archaeological investigation.

3. Archaeologists are really "detectives" of sorts. They must use their subject knowledge, coupled with scientific methodology, to determine as many pieces of information as they can about a particular excavation site or an individual artifact.

4. Most museums have an educational section which provides instruction and activities for teachers and students. These can test your students' powers of observation and reasoning. Remember that it is important for students to keep track of the information they have gathered.

Extended Activities:

Have students search these Web sites for additional information on the ancient world:

http://www.teachercreated.com/books/3804
Click on page 106, sites 3, 4, 5, 6, 7, 8, 9

Investigate the Ancient World

Name:_____

Using information gathered from Web sites, complete items 1–4 below. Then in small groups, do the activity at the bottom.

1. There are certain ways in which archaeologists investigate ancient world sites. One way is to look for pieces of ancient artifacts or other utensils. What are some advantages and disadvantages of different types of artifacts for providing information regarding the civilizations represented by these items?

   _____

   _____

   _____

2. What are some other information sources that archaeologists use? What do you consider to be the best sources of information about the Ancient World?

   _____

   _____

   _____

3. How did most of the major archeological information we currently know about get discovered?

   _____

   _____

   _____

4. How have improvements in modern technology (e.g. x-ray imaging, carbon-dating, etc.) helped us to expand our knowledge of the ancient world?

   _____

   _____

   _____

Activity:

Imagine you are visiting another country and you hear an announcement stating that a construction crew has just unearthed what looks like some sort of ancient temple. In a conversation with your traveling companions, the question is asked—"Why excavate?" Discuss in small groups first and then give reasons for and against excavation of the archaeological site.

Ancient Architecture

Name:_____

The ancient Greeks and Romans were responsible for some of the major developments in architecture. The Greeks contributed the idea of the *Golden Mean* and column construction. Some examples of classical Greek Architecture are The Parthenon, Apollo's Hall, and The British Museum in London, England.

Directions: Use the information you learned online to answer the questions below.

1. What is the *Golden Mean* ?

   _____

   _____

   _____

2. How does the Golden Mean affect architecture in general and Greek Architecture in particular?

   _____

   _____

   _____

   _____

3. What other construction advances were made by the Greeks?

   _____

   _____

   _____

4. What other architectural styles were developed by the Greeks?

   _____

   _____

   _____

Places—United States

The 50 States

Alaska

Hawaii

Washington D.C.

Cross Country Tour

U.S. Geography

Virtual Field Trips

 # The 50 States

Objective:

Make the study of the United States of America come alive by having students hone their research skills on the Internet. They will embrace this high-tech manner of gathering information versus the traditional flip through the encyclopedia.

Materials Needed:

- United States map
- note cards (optional)
- 1 copy of page 112 for each research group

Focus Web site:

http://www.teachercreated.com/books/3804
Click on page 110, sites 1 and 2

Keywords for Search Engines:

Students can use a search engine such as **Google.com** or **Yahooligans.com** (for younger students) to find more sites about the 50 states. They can type the name of the state they are studying in the search box.

Author's Note: Since this activity is open-ended, your students may need considerable time to access appropriate Web sites and gather information. Plan for each group to spend twenty to thirty minutes or more on the Internet. They may need additional class periods to complete their research.

 # The 50 States *(cont.)*

Pre-Internet Activity:

Post a map of the United States. Review the names of some of the states by calling them out and having volunteers show the class where that state is located on the map. Have the students share which state they would like to visit and tell why. Then explain to the class that they will have an opportunity to take a virtual vacation to their desired state with a teammate.

- Place students into teams of two by writing the names of the states and their matching capitals on note cards. (Write enough matches for each pair of students.) Randomly distribute the cards to students. They find classmates with the capital that matches the state on their cards. Classmates with matching cards act as an investigative team. The teams may then decide on a state to research, or you may wish to have them research the states on their cards.

Teaching the Lesson:

1. Students could spend literally hours linking to all the sites available to them on the Internet to complete their state research. Conduct a "Search Party" lesson to help students streamline their approach. With the class, begin on a home page of a favorite search engine. Type in the name of a state that none of the teams will research. Review all the categories from which to choose. Have the students list the ones they think are most pertinent to their investigation. Click on one of the categories, and then select a site of interest. If it does not look like what the students need, click <**Back**>. Alternatively, teachers can try some available links at the selected site to see if the students can find the answers to the research questions.

2. After the students have a research team and have chosen a state as their topic, they may begin researching on the Internet. Students may use the research guide on page 113 to help them refine their search and organize their information.

Extended Activities:

- Have the groups use their information to create a travel brochure for the state they researched. Post brochures on the wall outside of class for everyone to view.

- Have each member of the groups design a postcard from that state on a 5" x 8" (13 cm x 20 cm) blank note card. On the reverse side of the picture, they write a short note to their parents, using the information they learned from the Web sites to tell about the state. Have the students take them home and share what they learned.

- Have the groups devise a creative way to share the information they learned with the class (perhaps a diorama, poster, newscast, family vacation skit, or other unique means of communication). As the groups share their information, the audience takes notes. Collect the students' notes and make quiz cards. Play "State Jeopardy" one day during social studies.

State Research Guide

Name:_____

Directions: Use your favorite search engine. Type in the name of the state you are researching, and then select an appropriate category and links. Complete the information listed below.

State name _____

Important cities and events

City	Events
_____	_____
	_____
_____	_____
	_____
_____	_____

Things to see and do _____

_____

_____

_____

Attractions_____

_____

_____

_____

Other interesting information _____

_____

_____

_____

What one thing is most memorable about this state? _____

_____

_____

Aldaska

Objective:

Bald eagles soar past snow-topped peaks, and whales splash in open waters. Students can experience these sights and more as they gather information to learn about our 49th state: Alaska.

Materials Needed:

- world map or globe
- chalkboard
- drawing paper measuring 9" x 12" (23 cm x 30 cm) for each student
- 1 copy of page 116 for each student

Focus Web site:

http://www.teachercreated.com/books/3804

Click on page 113, site 1

Alternative Web sites:

http://www.teachercreated.com/books/3804

Click on page 113, sites 2, 3, 4, 5

Keywords for Search Engines:

Using your favorite search engine (such as **Google.com**), use keywords such as "travel Alaska," "Alaska culture," and "Alaska wildlife."

Alaska (cont.)

Pre-Internet Activity:

Using a world map or globe, show the class where they can find Alaska. Have the students tell some different ways they might travel there. If they were to visit, which means of transportation would they choose and why?

Alaska is very far north. Part of it extends into the Arctic Circle. Show the latitudinal line to the class. Have them tell what they think the climate is like this far north. Tell the students that they will have a chance to visit Alaska via the Internet. Here they will find out what kinds of animals inhabit this state as well as some interesting information about life in Alaska.

Teaching the Lesson:

1. Review the four seasons. Post the names of the four seasons on the chalkboard. Have the students share how the seasons are alike and different. Explain that in Alaska, winter and summer are as different as night and day! (They will find out the meaning of this when they visit the site.)

2. Distribute a copy of the activity from page 116 to each student.

3. Review the worksheet with the class before they begin.

4. Launch the Web site with the class, or have the students visit it in small groups. They will need to know how to use the **<Back>** link from the taskbar to return to the home page to complete the bottom half of the activity page.

5. After all of the students have completed the assignment, have them share which animals they drew pictures of on their worksheets. Make a class book of the variety of animals found in Alaska. Assign a different animal to each student or small groups of students. Have them use online or printed sources to discover facts about that animal. Have them write their information on a 9" x 12" (23 cm x 30 cm) sheet of drawing paper and include a full-page drawing of their creature. Combine all the pages to make one Alaskan wildlife book and place it at a reading center for all to enjoy during free-reading time.

Alaskan Wildlife

Arctic Region

Dall sheep

gray, killer, and beluga whales

moose

muskoxen

porcupine caribou

polar and grizzly bears

wolverines

wolves

140 different species of birds

Aleutian Islands Region

king salmon

halibut

fur seals

sea otters

waterfowl

 # Travel to Alaska

Name:_____

Directions: Use online sources to plan a trip to Alaska. Complete the sections below with details about your trip.

Native Alaskans are very important to Alaska's cultural heritage and present-day life. While you are in Alaska, you should learn more about this culture. You can go to a festival or visit a museum. In the space below, write about what you will do. Describe what you plan to see and why you are interested in seeing it.

_____

_____

_____

_____

What kind of wildlife would you like to see while you are in Alaska? Select two animals to research. In each of the boxes below, write the name of an Alaskan animal and draw a picture of it.

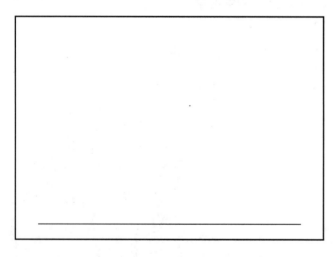

Find something else you would like to do in Alaska. For example, you might want to take a cruise or go sightseeing in an airplane. Write about what you are going to do and what you think it will be like.

_____

_____

_____

_____

Hawaii

Objective:

A virtual trip to this tropical paradise is only a click away. Students will dream of visiting the real thing after learning about the Hawaiian Islands and the Hawaiian alphabet and language.

Materials Needed:

- world map or globe
- chalkboard
- 1 copy of page 120 for each student
- brown construction paper measuring 12" x 18" (30 cm x 46 cm) for each student
- magazines
- drawing and writing paper

Focus Web site:

http://www.teachercreated.com/books/3804

Click on page 117, site 1

Alternative Web sites:

http://www.teachercreated.com/books/3804

Click on page 117, sites 2, 3

Keywords for Search Engines:

Using your favorite search engine (such as **Google.com**), use keywords Hawaii, Kauai, Oahu, Molokai, Lanai, and Maui.

Pre-Internet Activity:

Show the class where Hawaii is located on a map or globe. Demonstrate how to use the legend to determine the distance to the main island of Hawaii from your home state. Have students brainstorm sights they might see if they were to visit there.

Teaching the Lesson:

1. Compare the English alphabet with twenty-six letters to that of the Hawaiian language which has only twelve: a, e, i, o, u, h, k, l, m, n, p, and w. Have the students use these twelve letters to spell as many English words as possible. (You may wish to use this step as handwriting practice.) Explain that Hawaiian is a different language from English. Most Hawaiians speak English but still use their native language to communicate. The students will be excited by the opportunity to learn some genuine Hawaiian words when they visit the focus Web site.

2. Distribute a copy of page 120 to each student. Read over the directions with the class. Students will need to know how to return to a previous Web page. Demonstrate this task if they are unfamiliar with it.

3. As a class or in groups, have the students visit the Web site and complete the activity page.

4. Now that the students have visited the virtual Hawaii, they are probably ready to pack their bags and be on their way! Students demonstrate what they learned when they pack for a trip to Hawaii using a construction paper suitcase and pictures from magazines. Students cut handles in a folded sheet of 12" x 18" (30 cm x 46 cm) construction paper. Then they cut out items from magazines that they absolutely must take with them on their trip. After everyone has packed, have the students sit in a circle and share the items they packed.

5. Now the class is ready to take a trip to Hawaii. The students use what they learned about the land and its people to draw a picture of themselves in Hawaii. Students may use the Hawaiian words they learned to label items in their pictures.

Extended Activities:

- Many people would like to be able to change the name they have to something else. Here's a chance for students to do just that, and on the Internet, no less! If the students are interested in learning their names in Hawaiian, launch this Web site:

http://www.teachercreated.com/books/3804

Click on page 119, site 1

Once here, students read the brief summary, and then discover their Hawaiian names. They type their English names into the appropriate box and submit the entry. The computer will quickly return with Hawaiian substitutes.

Have each student write down his or her Hawaiian name, and then make a name tag to place on his or her desk for the remainder of the study of Hawaii. Have students write their Hawaiian names in big, bold letters on a 3" x 5" (8 cm x 13 cm) note cards, and then decorate them with pictures to describe themselves. Challenge the students (and yourself) to address their classmates by their Hawaiian names.

- Hawaii is a beautiful land one can only dream about when not actually experiencing it firsthand. Fortunately, Web sites exist to take Internet users away to paradise with the click of a button. Play some Hawaiian music and share some Hawaiian foods (pineapple and coconuts, for example) while you and your students share in the beauty and wonder of this enchanted land.

http://www.teachercreated.com/books/3804

Click on page 119, sites 2, 3

Hawaii Venn Diagram

Name: _____

Directions: In the Venn diagram below, compare and contrast Hawaii with your home state.

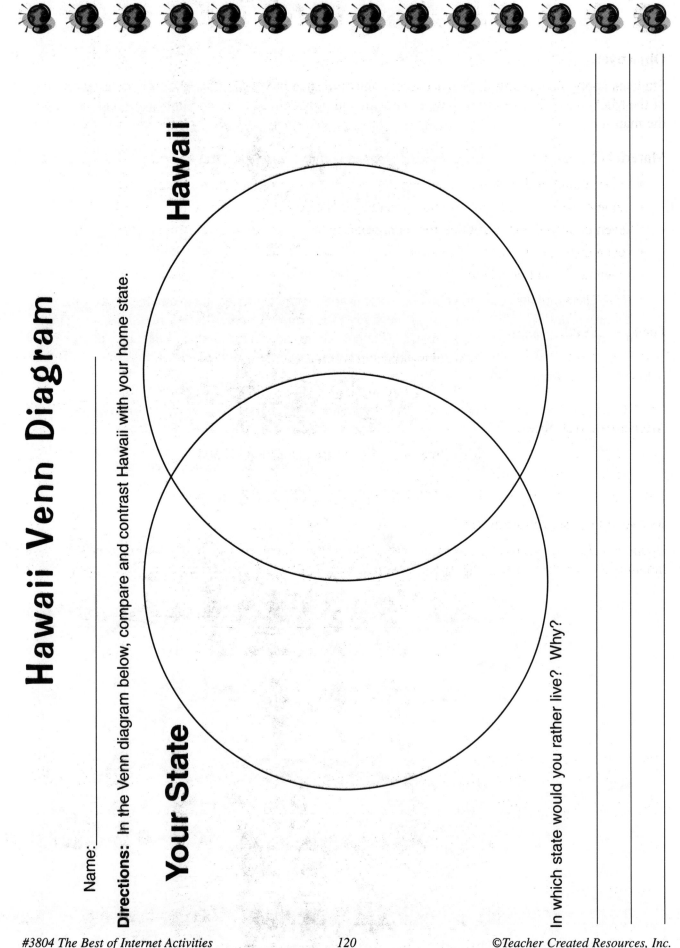

Hawaii

Your State

In which state would you rather live? Why?

_____
_____
_____

Washington, D.C.

Objective:

Students apply mapping skills to place a monument located in Washington, D.C., on a classroom map of the Mall area. They research their monument and provide a drawing and information to accompany the map.

Materials Needed:

- enlarge map of the Mall and surrounding area on poster board (see page 125)
- name of seven monuments written on note cards (see pre-Internet activity)
- seven copies of page 123, one for each group
- seven three-by-five-inch note cards
- seven additional note cards
- construction paper

Focus Web Site:

http://www.teachercreated.com/books/3804

Click on page 121, site 1

Alternative Web Sites:

http://www.teachercreated.com/books/3804

Click on page 121, sites 2, 3, 4

Keywords for Search Engines:

Using your favorite search engine (such as Google.com)use keywords such as "Washington, D.C. monuments," or the names of the specific monuments in the Mall area.

Washington, D.C. *(cont.)*

Pre-Internet Activity:

Enlarge the map of the Mall (label only the Capitol Building and Smithsonian Castle) onto a sheet of poster board. Display it along with the names of six monuments located in Washington, D.C.: (1) The Vietnam Veterans Memorial, (2) The Jefferson Memorial, (3) The Lincoln Memorial, (4) The White House, (5) Ford's Theatre, and (6) The Washington Monument. Have them speculate about the purpose of each monument. Explain to the students that they will have an opportunity to research each monument and discover where it is located on the map of the D.C. area.

Teaching the Lesson:

1. Divide the class into six groups, one to research each monument. Assign the groups a monument to research by randomly distributing the cards to the groups.

2. Distribute a copy of page 123 to each group. Allow the groups to access the Internet, gather their information, and mark the location of their monument by writing the number on the Mall map.

3. Students each transfer their sketch from the research guide onto a three-by-five-inch note card and cut it out around its outline. They secure it next to the location they marked on the map by folding the bottom edge of the picture back and gluing the tab to the poster board. Then they summarize the information they learned on an additional note card, including the name of the monument and the number. (Each monument on the map has a number next to it and a corresponding number on the card that gives details about it.)

4. Secure all the cards to one sheet of construction paper.

5. Display the completed three-dimensional Washington, D.C. map and cards in the library or on a table in the front office.

Extended Activities:

- Students may elect to create a simple three-dimensional model of their monument instead of simply using a paper drawing. Supply the students with the materials they need to complete this task. Follow the steps above to complete the map.

- Have the students reflect on their knowledge of American history to design and create a model of an original monument. They make a sketch or three-dimensional image of the monument and write a summary of its purpose, following the research guide on page 123. Students share their original monument with the class.

Washington, D.C. *(cont.)*

Name:_____

Directions: Go online to research a monument of Washington, D.C. Complete the information below.

Name of monument _____

Number on the card _____ Year it was erected or dedicated_____

Purpose of the monument _____

_____

_____

_____

A little bit of history_____

_____

_____

_____

Draw a picture of what this monument looks like.

More D.C. Links:

Students can have their fingers on the pulse of the nation by clicking on this site to get in touch with Congress. Find out what's happening today in the House and the Senate, or find out who your Congress members are and e-mail them with a valid concern or compliment.

http://www.teachercreated.com/books/3804

Click on page 124, site 1

Complement a study of specific sites in Washington by visiting these Web sites with the class.

http://www.teachercreated.com/books/3804

Click on page 124, sites 2, 3, 4, 5

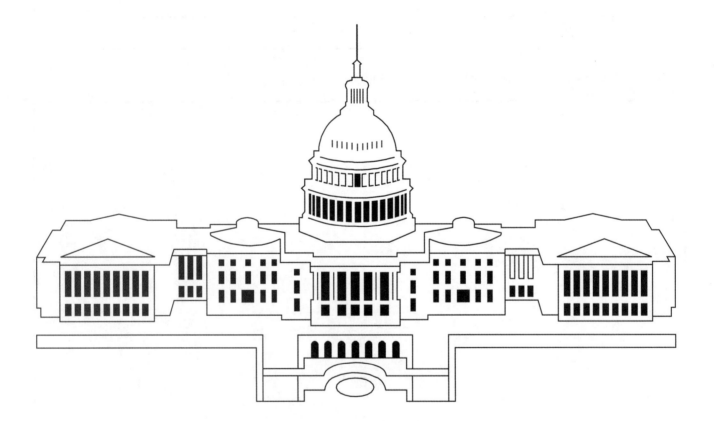

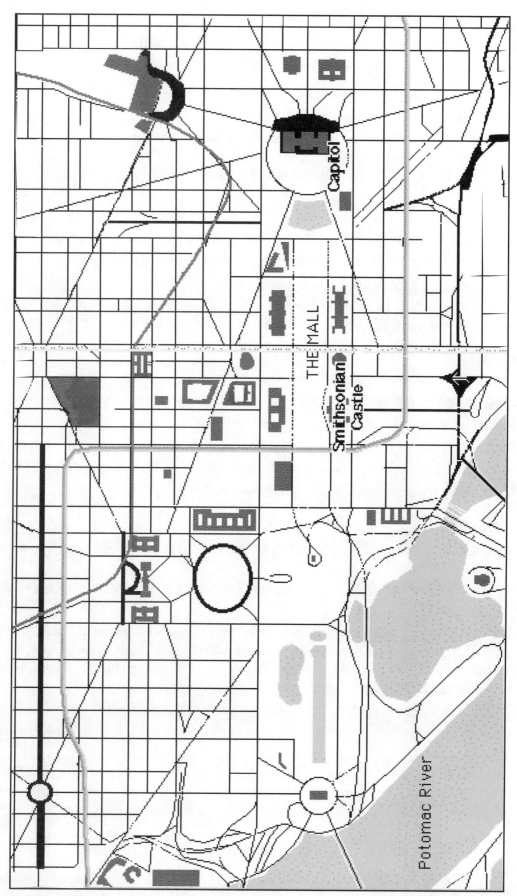

Cross Country Tour

Opening Comments:

Have you ever thought of taking your class on a cross country trip? With the Internet you can. In this lesson, students will take a trip across the country, keeping a log of their expenses and the places they visit.

Helpful Internet Sites:

http://www.teachercreated.com/books/3804

Click on page 126, sites 1, 2, 3, 4, 5

Setting the Stage:

- Explain the project to your students. If finding mileage is difficult, try AAA road maps.
- Browse the web sites with the class. Remind them of ways to navigate the Web.
- Review the work pages, guidelines, and grading criteria.
- Spend at least two periods completing a practice log with the class. You may want to put the student pages on an overhead and complete them together.

Student Procedure:

- Read the student guidelines for the project (page 127).
- Make sure you and your partner are familiar with information needed for the daily logs.
- Browse the Internet by beginning with suggested web sites.
- Keep complete records of the information you find in order to accurately fill in each daily log.
- Begin at one of the above sites. For hotels, follow the link to Concierge, Lodging, Hotels, etc.
- For mileage maps, try using the keyword "automap" or "mileage."

Special Considerations:

- This is meant to be a short activity (3–5 days) in length but can easily be expanded to last several weeks.
- If you decide to expand the project, have students purchase and keep track of meals using menus from local restaurants.
- In real life, there are no perfect travel days. There are usually unexpected expenses that occur. Use 3" x 5" (7.5 cm x 12.5 cm) cards to list several expenses and their costs. Examples include tire replacement, doctor visit, or evening entertainment. Each group chooses a card from the stack before they can finish their log.

Cross Country Tour (cont.)

Name:_____

Student Guidelines

You and your partner are to plan a trip across the country. You will keep a daily journal which will include the cities you visit, mileage, routes traveled, and lodging expenses. Begin with the listed web sites to help you in writing three sentences about one point of interest that you would visit each day in your travels.

Your round trip will last a minimum of three days with a maximum of five days. You must begin in your hometown and decide your own destination.

Each team will be given _____(currency) and your expenses may not exceed that amount, so plan carefully. Your daily journal sheet will include all detailed information concerning your expenses.

Planning Information

1. Due date _____

2. Team members _____,

   _____

3. Our destination city is: _____.

4. You may use a calculator to help with your expenses.
   BE VERY CAREFUL WITH YOUR MONEY.

5. You must stay in a hotel or motel each night. No camping.

6. If there is no point of interest to be found in the city you have chosen to lodge in, you may not stay there.

7. Keep track of the roads and mileage traveled on your trip.

8. Total expenses for the trip: _____

GRADING: Your grade will depend on two factors: (1) how much money you return with, and (2) the neatness and accuracy of the written work. Budgeting will account for 50% of your grade. The written portion is the other 50%. You and your partner will cooperate to complete *one set of journals and both will receive the same grade.*

Cross Country Tour *(cont.)*

Name:_____

Daily Log

Day Number:_____   Name: _____

Departure City: _____   Arrival City: _____

Web site used for information: _____

LODGING

Name of Motel/Hotel: _____

Web site used: _____

Address and phone number: _____

Price for the night (double occupancy): _____

MILEAGE

Miles traveled:_____

Roads/highways used today: _____

TOTAL OF DAY'S EXPENSES

Lodging expense: _____

Unexpected expenses: _____

Total of Day's expenses: _____

Balance brought forward: _____

Day's Expenses: _____

Funds Remaining: _____

Cross Country Tour (cont.)

Name:_____

Daily Log Part 2

Points of Interest

City: _____

Point of Interest (landmark):

_____

_____

_____

List three important facts about your point of interest. Use complete sentences with correct spelling and punctuation.

1. _____

    _____

    _____

2. _____

    _____

    _____

3. _____

    _____

    _____

U.S. Geography

Objective:

In part one of "Teaching the Lesson," students use traditional means to organize the details on one of seven regions of the United States and then reference a national park or geographic land form in that region. In part two, students apply their latitude and longitude skills to identify cities on a blank U.S. map.

Materials Needed:

- enlarge regions from page 131 onto poster board, chart, or bulletin board paper
- atlases, color relief maps of the United States, individual state maps
- large note cards
- one copy of page 132 for each student

Focus Web Sites:

   http://www.teachercreated.com/books/3804

      Click on page 130, sites 1, 2

Alternative Web Sites:

   http://www.teachercreated.com/books/3804

      Click on page 130, site 3

Keywords for Search Engines:

With your favorite search engine (such as **Google.com**), use as keywords the names of the national parks or geographic features that students are researching. Also use keywords "latitude," "longitude," and "altitude."

🌐 🌐 🌐 U.S. Geography (cont.) 🌐 🌐 🌐

Part One: Teaching the Lesson:

1. Enlarge each region of the United States from page 132 onto poster board or a large sheet of chart or bulletin board paper.

2. Divide the class into seven teams, one to research each region of the United States.

3. Students use atlases, color relief maps, and individual state maps to label the states and their capitals. They also mark major mountain ranges, deserts, rivers, lakes, swamps, marshes, etc. onto their enlarged region map. Finally, students identify and label three national parks in their region.

4. Have the students launch their favorite search engine home page (**Google.com** is recommended) and type in the name of a national park (e.g., Yosemite, Mammoth Cave) or geographic feature (e.g., Niagara Falls) from their region to search. They select an appropriate Web site from which to gather information about this area of interest and record the information onto a large note card.

5. Students share their research with the class, using their geographic region maps and Internet research.

6. Post the students' region maps and Internet research in the hall with the heading "Around the U.S.A."

Part Two: Teaching the Lesson:

1. Following a lesson on the concept of latitude and longitude, have students practice marking locations on a blank U.S. map. Distribute a copy of page 133 to each student. They launch the Web site and mark the locations of the cities on the map.

2. For additional practice, have the students use a U.S. map showing latitude and longitude lines to select two cities they think have about the same latitude and two others that share the same longitude. Have them access the focus Web site to discover if they were correct.

3. As a class, select a city in Alaska and compare its latitude to the cities on the activity page. Likewise, select a city in Hawaii to compare its longitude.

4. (Optional) When the students access the focus Web site to complete the activity page, have them record the populations of the cities as well. The students use this information to create a bar graph.

U.S. Geography *(cont.)*

Use these U.S. regions with part one from "Teaching the Lesson" on page 131.

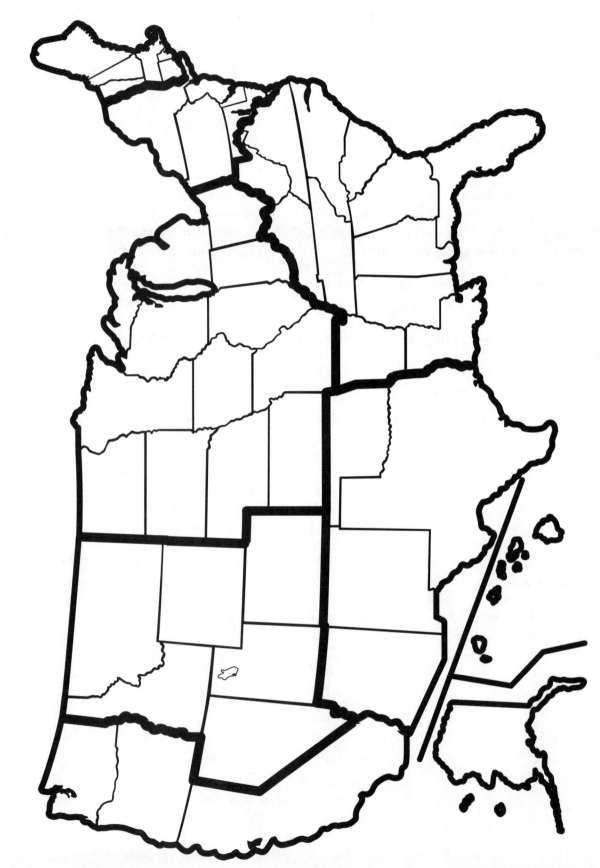

You Are Here

Directions: Find the latitude and longitude (in degrees) of each U.S. city below. Estimate and mark their locations on the map.

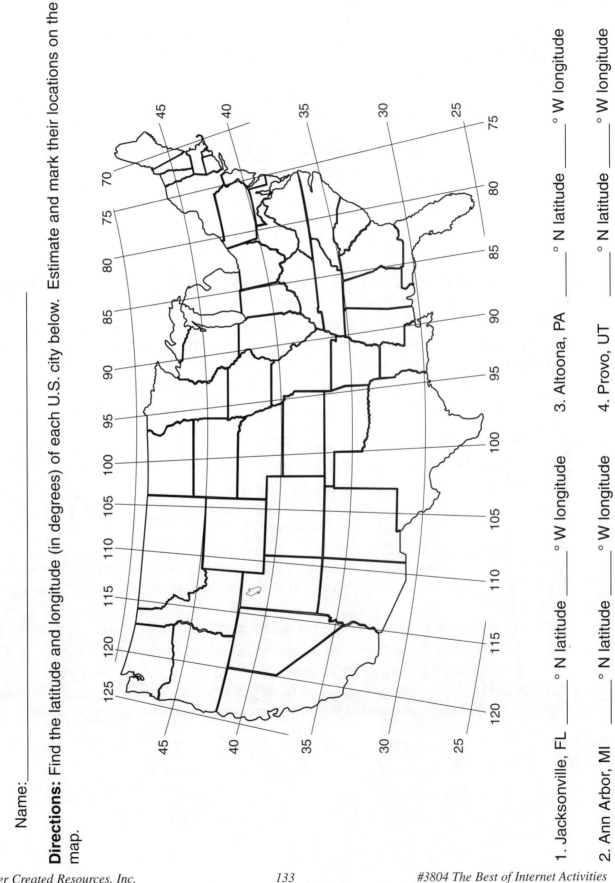

1. Jacksonville, FL _____ ° N latitude _____ ° W longitude

2. Ann Arbor, MI _____ ° N latitude _____ ° W longitude

3. Altoona, PA _____ ° N latitude _____ ° W longitude

4. Provo, UT _____ ° N latitude _____ ° W longitude

Virtual Field Trips

Opening Comments:

Would you like to take your students on more field trips, but (a) there are limited drivers for trips, and/or (b) the places you want to visit are too far away? Don't limit yourself or the curriculum. Review your lesson plans and take your class on a virtual field trip instead.

Some Helpful Internet Sites:

http://www.teachercreated.com/books/3804

Click on page 134, sites 1, 2, 3, 4, 5, 6, 7, 8

Keywords for Search Engines:

Using your favorite search engine (such as Google.com) use keywords such as the names of museums and national parks that students are interested in visiting.

Setting the Stage:

- Choose the place you want students to visit. Find a tour that fits into a theme you are studying or a place that is of special interest to your students.
- Make bookmarks of sites to visit or put the URLs on cards at the computer.
- Complete a KWL chart with your class. (See page 179.) This preview can provide a good springboard for student questions.
- Copy and review the Field Trip Logs with students.

Procedure:

- The teacher or students decide on two questions to answer from the field trip visit and write these on their Field Trip Logs.
- Students work alone or in pairs to view a field trip site.
- Children fill in the answers to complete their Field Trip Logs.

Special Considerations and Other Options:

- Post completed papers on a bulletin board of work related to the field trip topic. For instance, if the White House is being studied, post Field Trip Logs that answer student questions about the White House.
- If printers are available, have students print information from the Web sites they visited.
- Print-screens of Web site pictures can be a great addition to a class book about the unit of study or to illustrate information gathered by the students.
- For younger students, or those who have difficulty reading and writing, assign a scavenger hunt of sorts. In this case, students need to find certain pictures, sounds, or images at the site.

Virtual Field Trips *(cont.)*

Name:_____

Field Trip Log

1. Write down two questions about a place you would like to visit.
2. Go to the site and look for the answers to your questions. Write the answers below.

SITE:_____

URL:_____

Question #1: _____

_____

_____

Answer #1: _____

_____

Question #2: _____

_____

Answer #2: _____

_____

_____

International

The Blarney Stone

Japan

Mexico: The Mayas

Africa: On Safari

China

Online Travel Log

The Blarney Stone

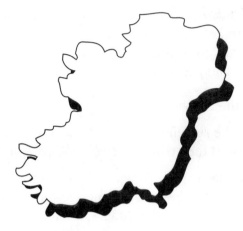

Objective:

Nearly all young people have the gift of gab—and that's no blarney! Complement your unit on Ireland by introducing this legendary part of Irish history.

Materials Needed:

- chalkboard
- 1 copy of page 140 for each student

Focus Web site:

http://www.teachercreated.com/books/3804

Click on page 137, site 1

Alternative Web site:

http://www.teachercreated.com/books/3804

Click on page 137, site 2

General Ireland Sites:

http://www.teachercreated.com/books/3804

Click on page 137, sites 3, 4, 5

Keywords for Search Engines:

Using your favorite search engine (such as **Google.com**), use keywords such as "Ireland" and "Blarney Stone."

Pre-Internet Activity:

Have the students list some good luck charms or actions that are supposed to bring good luck. What are some other "superstitions" people believe? Are they really true? Tell the class that they will have an opportunity to visit Ireland's legendary Blarney Stone, which is supposed to give a person the gift of "eloquence and persuasive flattery" (or gab) if you kiss it.

Teaching the Lesson:

1. Have the students share what they know about castles. List the students' ideas on the board. Tell them that they will visit Blarney Castle in Ireland on the Internet.

2. Distribute a copy of page 141. Read the directions with the students. Launch the Web site with the class or allow the students to work in small groups. If working as a class, have students volunteer to read the paragraphs and summarize what they've read before going on.

3. The legend of the famous Blarney Stone says that people who kiss it will be granted the gift of gab. Unfortunately, visitors must lean over backwards on a banister to reach it. Just for fun, students may visit the Web site which allows viewers to kiss the Stone electronically.

http://www.teachercreated.com/books/3804

Click on page 138, site 1

Students read the legend, and then take turns clicking the mouse to pretend-kiss the image of the stone on the screen. Have students keep tabs on their classmates. At the end of the day, discuss whether or not the electronic kiss worked. Did anyone feel more likely to talk? Did they notice anyone else talking more than usual?

4. Have the students write a tale to explain an original American folk legend. Students think of an object, an action one must do to that object, and the outcome of the action. Then they write a tale telling how that legend came to be.

Example:

Object:	Bag of rice
Action:	Shake it
Outcome:	Become a good dancer

The Blarney Stone *(cont.)*

Extended Activities:

- Remember the "pet rock?" Students can take a piece of Ireland home with them in the form of their own pet rock. Of course, it won't have the magical gifts of the *real* Blarney Stone, but students will enjoy their rocks just the same. Have the students hunt outside for a suitable rock. Use a hot glue gun to secure eyes (from the craft department) on the rock for the students. Then they can use acrylic paints, permanent markers, or craft paints to finish decorating their rocks. Have the students name them and tell what kind of good fortune they bring.

- Irish myths and legends abound in Ireland. Older students may wish to investigate an authentic Irish myth and share it with the class. The following Web sites offer viewers a chance to read up on Irish myths.

http://www.teachercreated.com/books/3804

Click on page 139, sites 1, 2

http://www.teachercreated.com/books/3804

Click on page 139, site 3

Name:_____

Directions: Read about the Blarney Stone and Blarney Castle. Imagine that you have gone on a trip to Ireland and kissed the Blarney Stone. Write a story about what happened to you afterward. Did you get the gift of gab?

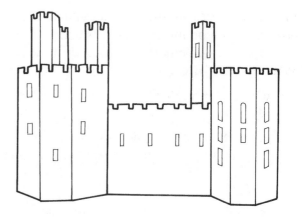

_____

_____

_____

_____

_____

_____

_____

_____

_____

_____

_____

_____

_____

_____

_____

_____

_____

_____

_____

Japan

Objective:

Students will treasure their virtual visit to the "Land of the Rising Sun" by making a kimono-shaped booklet filled with interesting facts about Japan.

Materials Needed:

- world map or globe
- traceable pattern of kimono from page 144
- Oak tag or posterboard for patterns
- 1 copy of page 144 for each student
- chart paper or sentence strips
- three sheets of plain white copy paper per student
- two 9" x 12" (23 cm x 30 cm) sheets of colorful construction paper per student

Focus Web site:

http://www.teachercreated.com/books/3804

Click on page 141, site 1

Alternative Web sites:

http://www.teachercreated.com/books/3804

Click on page 141, sites 2, 3

Keywords for Search Engines:

Using your favorite search engine (such as **Google.com**), use keywords such as "Japan," "Origami," and "Haiku."

Japan (cont.)

Pre-Internet Activity:

On a world or globe, show the class where Japan is located. Explain that it is an island nation which is considered part of the continent of Asia. List some other countries students may have heard of that are also found in Asia. Explain that although many Americans may think the cultures of Asian countries are similar, each country is quite culturally diverse. Tell the class that they will have a chance to learn about the Japanese culture on the Internet.

Teaching the Lesson:

1. Make a copy of the kimono outline from page 144. Use it to make several traceable patterns on oak tag or poster board.

2. Assign groups of three to four students to act as research teams. Each team will be responsible for accessing the focus Web site and discovering one interesting fact about Japan.

3. Distribute page 144 to each student. Explain that a kimono is a traditional Japanese robe-like garment usually made of silk or cotton with intricate embroidery. The teams work together to search the links from the destination URL for interesting facts about Japan. They write their information on the lines in the kimono.

4. After all the teams have completed their assignment, have one person from each group share his or her interesting fact with the class. Write the students' sentences on chart paper or sentence strips. Post the facts where everyone can see them.

5. The students then cut out their Kimono from the activity page. They use the patterns to trace three additional Kimonos on white paper and two from colorful construction paper. Using the other teams' sentences from the chart, each student chooses four facts and writes one on each blank kimono. Then they illustrate the sentences. Secure the four information pages about Japan inside the construction paper cut outs. Students decorate the covers of their booklets with Japanese-style designs and include a title, such as "All About Japan." Now each student has a unique booklet telling four interesting facts about Japan.

6. Have the students share their facts with a peer reader or adult volunteer. Students then take their booklets home to share the information with their parents.

Extended Activities:

- As part of a unit about Japan, have the students access these sites telling about haiku, (traditional Japanese poetry) and origami (the art of paper folding).

http://www.teachercreated.com/books/3804

Click on page 143, site 1, 2

The art of paper folding can be tricky for young learners with small fingers. One suggestion is to access a web site with only a few students at one time since the directions may be too confusing to try to conduct an origami project with the whole class.

Japan *(cont.)*

Name:_____

Directions: Learn about Japan on the Internet. Then, on the lines below, write a paragraph about what you learned.

Mexico: The Mayas

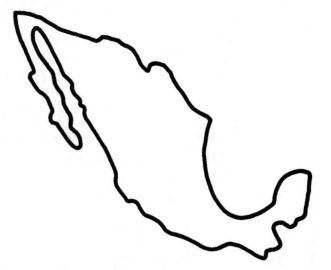

Objective:

The ruins are all that are left of this ancient civilization, but students can bring its spirit alive as they study the architecture of the Mayan culture in the Yucatan Peninsula.

Materials Needed:

- map of world or Western Hemisphere
- 1 copy of page 148 for each student

Focus Web site:

http://www.teachercreated.com/books/3804

Click on page 145, site 1

Alternative Web sites:

http://www.teachercreated.com/books/3804

Click on page 145, sites 2, 3

Keywords for Search Engines:

Using your favorite search engine (such as **Google.com**), use keywords such as "Mayas," "Mayan Culture," or "Chichen Itza."

Pre-Internet Activity:

Explain to the students that three groups of Native Americans (the Mayas, Incas, and Aztecs) inhabited the lands south of the United States. On a world map or map of the Western Hemisphere, mark the general locations of these civilizations with colorful dots. Explain that their civilizations died out long ago, but the ruins of their great cities still stand. Tell the students that they will have an opportunity to learn more about one of these peoples, the Mayas, as they visit a site devoted to educating students about their history.

Civilization	Region Inhabited
Aztecs	Central and Southern Mexico
Incas	Primarily Peru and Other Andean Regions of South America
Mayas	Primarily in the Yucatan Peninsula (and Other Regions Of Mexico), Guatemala, Belize, and Honduras

Teaching the Lesson:

1. Ask the students to imagine a world with no electricity, engines, or other modern technology. Now ask them to describe how they might go about building a small house, a large apartment building or a massive skyscraper. Explain that the Mayas did not construct buildings like those of today, but rather erected large stone pyramids and entertainment complexes in their cities—all without the use of modern-day equipment. Tell the students they will have a chance to view some Mayan architecture on the Internet.

2. Distribute a copy of the activity on page 148. Read over the directions with the class. Launch the Web site together.

3. Allow groups of three or four students at a time to visit the Web site and complete the activity page.

4. Have the students share their example of Puuc architecture with the class. Revisit the site as a class and compare what the students learned about Puuc architecture to the Toltec-Maya architecture.

5. Try linking to some other Mayan civilizations of interest. Have the students list similarities and differences among the different tribes.

Extended Activities

- Have the students create a model of a Mayan pyramid, using the pattern on page 150. The students color and decorate the outside faces to resemble the Mayan style, and then follow the directions to make a pyramid.

- The Mayas are known for their powerful command of mathematics. Students can learn their counting system by visiting this site:

http://www.teachercreated.com/books/3804

Click on page 147, site 1

View the chart depicting the Mayan symbols and words for numbers one through twenty. Can students see the patterns the Mayas used to graphically represent numbers? What do they think the graphic symbol for thirty might have been?

Write the Arabic numerals 1 through 20 on 2" x 2" (5 cm x 5 cm) squares of construction paper and matching Mayan symbols for these numbers on cards measuring 2" x 3" (5 cm x 8 cm). Place the matching set of numerals and symbols at a center for students to practice matching.

Mexico: The Mayas *(cont.)*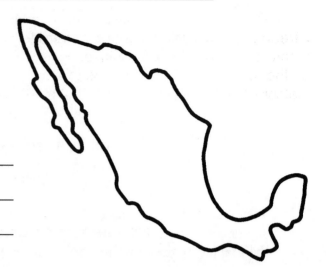

Name:_____

Directions: Use the information you learned online to complete this activity page.

Mayan Life:

What did you learn about the life of the Mayan people?

_____

_____

_____

_____

_____

_____

_____

Mayan Architecture:

Draw an example of Mayan architecture in the box below.

_____

_____

_____

_____

_____

Mayan Mystery:

You may have read on one of the websites for this activity that the Mayan civilization essentially disappeared. What do you think happened to them?

_____

_____

_____

_____

_____

A Mayan Pyramid

Name:_____

Directions: Decorate the sides of the pyramid. Cut on the dotted lines. Fold on the solid lines. Glue the tabs to their matching pieces.

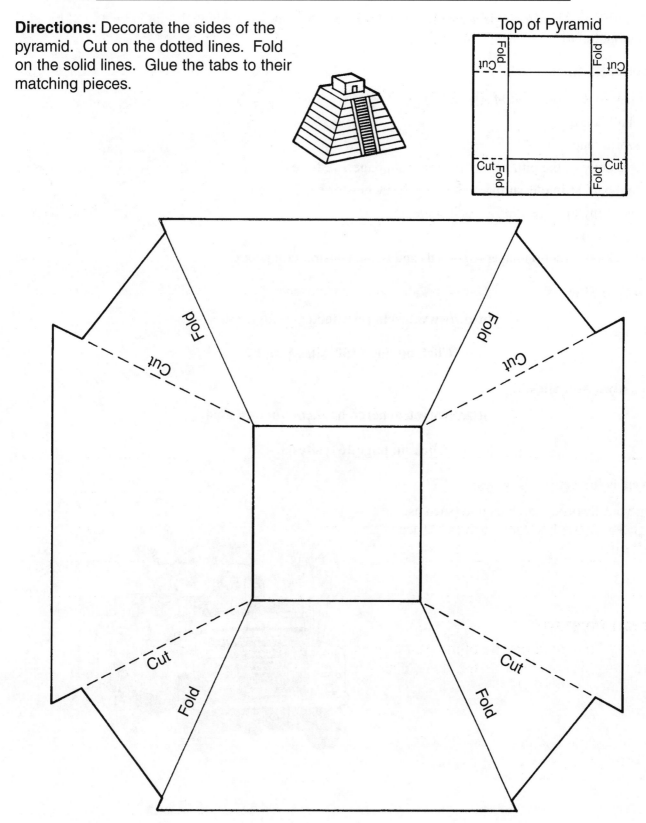

Top of Pyramid

Fold
Cut
Fold
Cut
Fold
Cut
Fold
Cut

Fold
Cut
Fold
Cut

Fold
Cut
Fold
Cut

Cut
Fold

Africa: On Safari

Objective:

The wilds of an African jungle are merely a click away when students don their pith helmets and travel on a virtual Safari.

Materials Needed:

- map of the continent of Africa
- chalkboard
- world map
- one copy of the pith helmet pattern from page 152 for each student
- tagboard strip measuring about 2 by 26 inches for each student
- one copy of page 153 for each student
- note cards
- black construction paper (optional) and white construction paper

Focus Web Site:

http://www.teachercreated.com/books/3804

Click on page 150, sites 1 and 2

Alternative Web Sites:

http://www.teachercreated.com/books/3804

Click on page 151, sites 3, 4, 5

Keywords for Search Engines:

Using your favorite search engine (such as **Google.com**), use keywords such as "Africa virtual safari."

Africa: On Safari (cont.)

Pre-Internet Activity:

Display a map of the continent of Africa. Have the students identify some countries with which they may be familiar and show their locations on the map. Have the students name some animals they might see if they were to go on an African safari. List the names of the animals on the chalkboard. Explain that although we think of elephants as being from Africa, they, like much of the wildlife, are only found in specific regions, not over the entire continent. Tell the students that they will have a chance to track some animals on an African safari on the Internet in one specific location of Africa called Okavango.

Teaching the Lesson:

1. Review these geographic terms: delta, river, lake. Have the students define each term and give an example of each, using a world map. Explain that the region of Africa they will be visiting is part of a delta. They will learn more specific information when they visit the Web site.

2. What African safari would be complete without the appropriate gear? Have the students color and decorate the pith helmet outline from page 152. Secure it to a headband measuring 2 inches high by 26 inches long, and staple to fit around the students' heads.

3. Distribute a copy of page 153 to each student. As a class or in small groups, have the students follow the directions to complete the activity page. Students may need assistance using the map scale to complete questions 3 through 5.

4. Divide the class into six groups to further research the six animals whose tracks they identified: cheetah, wild dog, pangolin, lechwe, crocodile, and hippopotamus. The students write their information on a large note card or create a report in a word processing program. Then they make a long trail of tracks cut from black construction paper and glued to a strip of white construction paper measuring 18 by 6 inches. (Students may also simply draw the tracks onto the paper strip.) Post the students' tracks and information in the hallway with the title, "Mysterious Tracks." Challenge the students from other classes as well as visitors to match the tracks with the correct African animal.

Africa: On Safari (cont.)

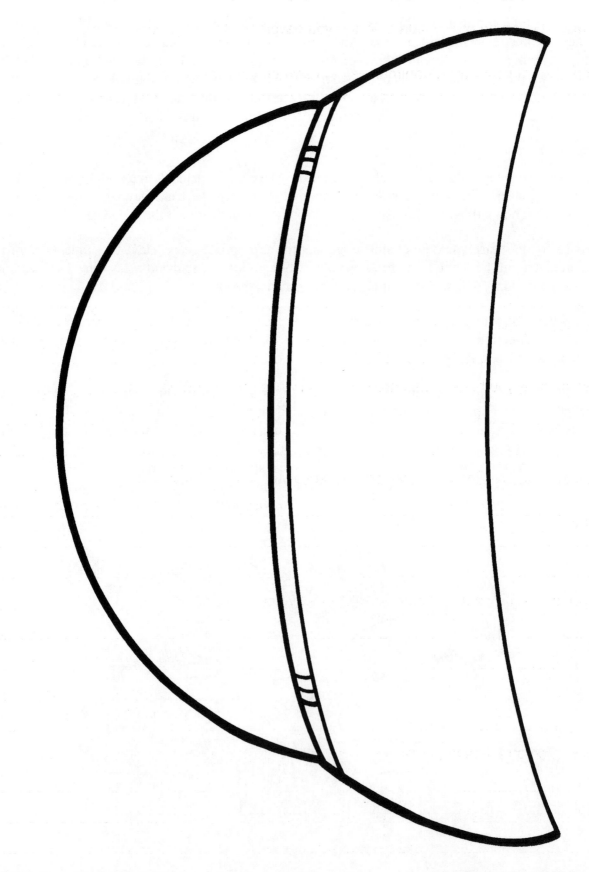

On Safari

Name:_____

Directions: Go on an online safari. When you have completed the safari, complete this activity page.

Draw a picture of your favorite animal that you saw on your safari.

What is the name of this animal?

_____

Name something you have to be careful to avoid while you are on your safari.

_____

_____

Describe three interesting facts you learned while you were on your safari.

_____

_____

_____

Would you like to go on a real safari? Why or why not?

_____

_____

_____

If you did go on a real safari, what would you really like to see?

_____

_____

_____

Africa: On Safari *(cont.)*

Extended Activities:

- Students may enjoy an authentic African tale on the Internet. This full-length story is available for pleasure reading complete with colorful illustrations. Spend oral reading time one day sharing this mesmerizing tale with the students.

http://www.teachercreated.com/books/3804

Click on page 154, site 1

- Students can observe the animals on safari through faux binoculars. Encourage the students to view the world through this perspective by bringing in sets of binoculars clearly labeled with their names. Spend some time outdoors viewing wildlife (or still life) through the lenses, and then give students a copy of the pattern below to sketch their observations as seen through the binoculars. Post them on a bulletin board entitled "A Bird's-Eye View."

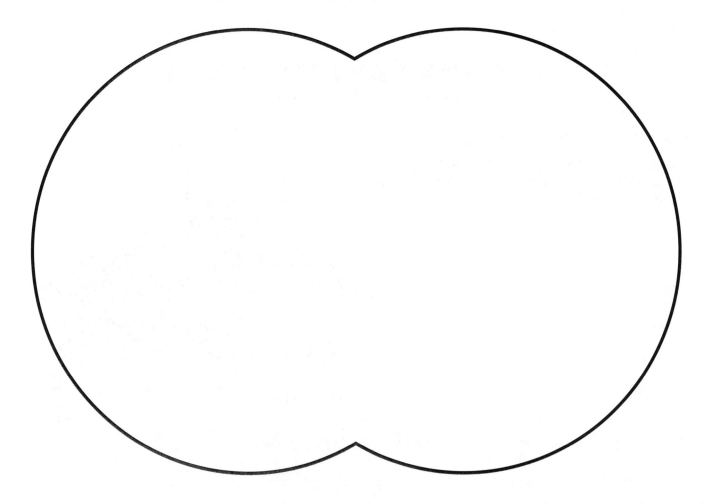

 # China

Objective:

Students consider their reactions if they were to live in an unfamiliar country. Then they learn how the tendency for groups with common backgrounds to live together, excluding others, affects China's culture. They apply new vocabulary to their study of China and reference additional cultural and ethnic points of interest.

Materials Needed:

- chalkboard
- one copy of page 157 for each student
- large sheet of drawing paper
- additional drawing paper (optional)

Focus Web Site:

http://www.teachercreated.com/books/3804

Click on page 155, site 1

Alternative Web Sites:

http://www.teachercreated.com/books/3804

Click on page 155, sites 2, 3, 4

Keywords for Search Engines:

Using your favorite search engine (such as **Google.com**), use keywords such as "China" and "Chinese culture."

China (cont.)

Pre-Internet Activity:

Review the students' nationalities. Make a master list of them on the chalkboard. Discuss how the students, as Americans, would feel if they went to live in another country (Portugal, for example). What are some problems the students think might arise? What would help make their transition a little easier? Explain that when a large number of people immigrate to a specific country, they often form small communities of their own nationalities. Have the students work in small groups to brainstorm a list of pros and cons for this tactic. Have them share their ideas with the class. Explain to the students that in China a similar situation occurred, and they will have a chance to read about the diversity of populations inhabiting China.

Teaching the Lesson:

1. Post these terms and definitions on the chalkboard.

minority	group of people who make up less than half of the total population
autonomy	self-governing
compact	occupying a small area

   Discuss how each term relates to the student classroom population. (The number of people who have a horse might be in the *minority*; when groups get together to work, they do so in a modified state of *autonomy*; closet space might be *compact*, etc.)

2. Distribute a copy of page 157 to each student. As a class or in small groups, have the students access the focus Web site and complete the activity page.

3. Review the vocabulary words from step 1. Now have the students share how the terms relate to their study of China's culture. Distribute a large sheet of drawing paper to the students. They fold the paper twice to make three sections and then write one term in each section and illustrate its meaning.

🌐 🌐 🌐 The Chinese Culture 🌐 🌐 🌐

Name:_____

Directions: Use websites to find the information needed to complete this activity sheet.

1. Write a word in Chinese. _____

   What does this word mean in English? _____

2. When is the Chinese new year this year? _____

   What year is it by the Chinese calendar? _____

3. Why do the people of China celebrate the new year on different days every year?

   _____

   _____

4. Dragons are an important part of Chinese culture. Write down the names of two dragons and at least one interesting fact about each.

   • _____

   _____

   • _____

   _____

5. What do Yin and Yang stand for?

   _____

   _____

6. Draw the Yin Yang symbol in the box below.

China (cont.)

Extended Activities:

- Display a country map of China. Have the students take turns reviewing the map to identify any major cities, points of interest, or general geography information. Divide the class into nine groups. Assign the groups a different "hot spot" to access. (See listing below.) They write what it is and draw a picture of it on a three-by-five-inch note card. Then each group shares the information about its "hot spot" and tapes the card to the appropriate location on the map (north, south, central, etc.).

Hainan Island	Forbidden City	Temple of Heaven
Huangshan Mountain	Shanghai	Terra-cotta Army
The Great Wall	Hong Kong	Tiananmen Square

- Introduce students to the Chinese art of paper cutting by first visiting this site to view some actual cuts and then designing and creating their own.

http://www.teachercreated.com/books/3804

Click on page 158, site 1

To make a paper cut, each student will need a sheet of black and a sheet of white construction paper. The students fold the white paper and make several random cuts to remove small pieces of the paper. When they are done cutting, they mount the white paper onto the black paper. If desired, the students may trim the black paper to match the outline of the white paper.

- *The Year of the Boar and Jackie Robinson* by Bette Bao Lord is a story that tells of one young Chinese girl's confusion as she struggles to adjust to American culture and society. Share this story with the class. Upon its completion, visit this Web site about the Chinese zodiac and see if events from the story matched the boar's personality. Students may also wish to spend some time discovering their own Chinese zodiac animals. Chances are most students were born during the same two consecutive years. Students may access the information by themselves, or you may wish to access the Web site as a class.

http://www.teachercreated.com/books/3804

Click on page 158, site 2

  # Online Travel Log

Opening Comments:

This activity can be as broad as your imagination allows. In this case, students will choose a country and find specific information before writing a final paper. The other possibilities are almost limitless, but look under "Special Considerations" for some more options.

Helpful Internet Sites:

http://www.teachercreated.com/books/3804

Click on page 159, sites 1, 2, 3, 4

Setting the Stage:

- Give students the worksheet and project guidelines on pages 160–162.

- Discuss the requirements for the project. Be sure to review what you mean by "final draft."

- Give students a set time to browse for helpful links.

- Model how to copy and paste site URLs into a file for future reference.

- Have students keep a map and written list of locations they visit in their writing.

Procedure:

- Students will visit suggested Web sites and take notes on their worksheets.

- Begin the rough draft—including at least three Web site links.

- Have students peer edit the papers, possibly checking for accessibility of the noted sites.

- Students will complete a final draft of their assignment.

Special Considerations:

- Spread the news by sending (posting) results to mailgroups to which your students subscribe.

- Consider also sending student work to the webmasters of sites visited.

- Some other options may be to have students:

  1. Write a travel log.

  2. Write a fictional travel adventure.

  3. Keep the travel records for an imaginary agent, (e.g., *Carmen SanDiego.*)

  4. Write about factual travel on a limited topic (i.e. a trip across America, explore the 13 colonies, tour the ancient worlds).

  5. Turn the facts into a bit of historical fiction.

Online Travel Log (cont.)

Student Guidelines:

In this project you will be asked to choose a country to research. Use the Tourist Data Form to take notes while you are online.

Criteria for Project:

- A minimum of three Web links are included.

- A map of areas (cities, states, etc.) visited is included.

- The "Tourist Data Form" is completely filled out.

- URLs are copied and pasted to a folder for future use.

- Saved URLs are copied and pasted from a folder to the location box to visit a site.

- Final draft is a minimum of one page written information about the country.

Pieces of the Project:

- ❏ Research online and complete the Tourist Data Form. Be sure to keep a map of your visit as well.

- ❏ As you research, copy the URLs you used to a folder for your next visit.

- ❏ When offline, write a paper including all the information you found on the Web. Be sure to include proper paragraph format and correct spelling.

- ❏ Have a friend or your teacher correct your paper for any errors.

- ❏ Rewrite your country paper.

- ❏ Make a neat final copy of your map as well.

🌐🌐🌐 Online Travel Log (cont.) 🌐🌐🌐

Name:_____

Online Travel Data Form

Choose a country to visit and then complete the form below.

1. What continent is the country on? _____

2. What are the land boundaries? _____

   _____

   _____

3. What water areas does this country claim? _____

   _____

   _____

4. List the natural resources. _____

   _____

   _____

5. What is the climate like?_____

   _____

   _____

6. Tell about the terrain. _____

   _____

   _____

7. Make a bar graph on the back of this page showing the population of the chosen country.

Name:_____

Online Travel Data Form *(cont.)*

9. Describe the type of government in place in this country. _____

    _____

    _____

10. List the exports and imports. _____

11. What language is spoken in _____ (name of country)?

    _____

12. What form of currency is used? _____

    _____

13. Name three major cities located in this country._____

    _____   _____

14. The Eiffel Tower and the Great Wall of China are two well known landmarks. Are there any internationally known landmarks in your chosen country? If so, what are they? And why were they constructed?

    _____

    _____

    _____

    _____

    _____

    _____

    _____

    _____

Science

Animals

Healthy Choices

Weather Browser

Scientists' Gazette

Going Buggy!

Love That Lava

Rain Forest Stations

 # Animals

Opening Comments:

Put a new twist on short report writing. Invite your students onto the World Wide Web to find out about animals in the world. Using this cooperative group format may give reports in the classroom a truly new dimension.

Some Helpful Internet Sites:

http://www.teachercreated.com/books/3804

Click on page 164, sites 1, 2, 3, 4

Keywords for Search Engines:

Using your favorite search engine (such as **Google.com**), use as keywords the names of animals students are researching.

Setting the Stage:

- Brainstorm animals to research. Consider assigning reports on an animal population that fits into a curricular theme (i.e. rain forests, oceans, Arctic birds).

- Set short term deadlines for portions of the project (research completed, rough draft, final draft, and so on).

- Review the project and cooperative group rubric on page 165.

- Remind your students of the deadlines. You may want to post these near the computer.

- Encourage students to search out other links for information on diverse animal populations.

Procedure:

- Students review the guidelines on page 165.

- Students complete online research using the Group Project Animal Research Form page 166 for note-taking.

- Following the requirements on the Student Guidelines page, students write, practice, and present their information to the class.

Special Considerations:

As in all cooperative group situations, be aware of who has decided to work together or whom you place in a group. Try to make the groups as successful a combination as possible.

Animals *(cont.)*

Name:_____

Student Guidelines

Information to be included:

1. Where the animal lives (habitat).

2. What the animal eats.

3. How the animal protects itself.

4. Who the animal's enemies are.

5. Adaptations made by the animal to live in the environment.

Requirements:

- Each group will produce one poster with the information on their animal. The poster will include one question answered by each person, and one drawing or picture per person (this could be of the animal, its environment, its food or enemies).

- The group will make a presentation to the class, explaining the information on the poster.

Grading:

Posters will be graded on the following:

1. Includes all the required information.

2. Uses complete sentences, correct spelling, and punctuation.

3. Shows neatness and color. (Neatness includes legibility.)

Presentations will be graded on the following:

1. Includes all the information on the poster.

2. Group members are able to answer further questions on your animal.

3. Speaking is loud and clear.

Working Together:

1. The group will decide who will answer which question. They will also decide how the poster will be designed.

2. Each person will research his/her question, fill in the forms, and get them approved by the teacher.

3. Each person will write his/her information on a separate piece of paper and add it to the group poster.

4. Each person will create a drawing and add it to the poster.

5. Each person will plan and practice the presentation.

6. Each person will present the information to the class.

Animals (cont.)

Name:_____

Animal Research Form

Visit three zoos online. Use the form below to take notes about the animal you are studying.

Zoo _____ City, State (Country)_____

URL _____ Animal searched for: _____

Scientific name (genus/species name)_____

Habitat: _____

_____

Food:_____

_____

Enemies:_____

_____

How does the animal protect itself? _____

_____

Are there any special adaptations of this animal to its environment? If so, what are they?

_____

_____

_____

_____

Is this an endangered species? How long has it been on the endangered list? Why has this species been put in jeopardy?

_____

_____

_____

_____

Animals (cont.)

Rough Draft Form

Read page 165 (student guidelines) and then fill in the form below.

1. The _____ (animal) lives in _____.

2. The _____ eats _____

_____, _____,

and _____.

3. This animal catches its food by _____

_____

_____.

4. The _____ protects itself by _____ and by

_____

_____.

5. Enemies of the _____ include_____,

_____, and _____.

6. The _____ have adapted to their
environment by

_____ and _____

_____.

 # Healthy Choices

Opening Comments:
Making healthy food choices is a life-long skill. This activity is one means of better teaching our students just what some of those food and life style choices can be.

Some Helpful Internet Sites:

http://www.teachercreated.com/books/3804

Click on page 168, sites 1, 2, 3, 4

Setting the Stage:
- Review the Food Guideline Pyramid with your students.
- Discuss the effects on our bodies of the foods we eat.
- Copy and hand out the Menu Choices worksheets on pages 169 and 170.
- It is suggested that this activity be graded on completeness of the worksheet, variety in food choices, as well as accurate spelling and calculations.
- Review your grading criteria with the class and post the rubric.

Procedure:
- Students will read the directions on the Menu Choices worksheets.
- Students will browse through at least one Web site to help them with their menus.
- Worksheets are completed according to the directions and grading criteria.

Special Considerations:
- This activity is meant to supplement a more complete health unit.
- Visit the suggested Web sites for more health resources and references.
- You may want to contact your local Dairy Council for a unit on foods.

Healthy Choices (cont.)

Name:_____

Menu Choices

1. Visit at least two different Web sites to access health information about suggested food requirements.

2. Create a menu for one person for a single day. Foods chosen must follow the current guidelines in the Food Guide Pyramid.

3. Using food labels, total up the amount of fat and sodium in the menu choices. Check to make sure that these totals are at or below the suggested daily amounts.

Breakfast			
Food	**# Servings**	**Fat**	**Sodium**
_____	_____	_____	_____
_____	_____	_____	_____
_____	_____	_____	_____
_____	_____	_____	_____
_____	_____	_____	_____
_____	_____	_____	_____
_____	_____	_____	_____
_____	_____	_____	_____
_____	_____	_____	_____
_____	_____	_____	_____
	Total:	_____	_____

Healthy Choices (cont.)

Menu Choices

Lunch			
Food	**# Servings**	**Fat**	**Sodium**
_____	_____	_____	_____
_____	_____	_____	_____
_____	_____	_____	_____
_____	_____	_____	_____
_____	_____	_____	_____
_____	_____	_____	_____
_____	_____	_____	_____
	Total:	_____	_____

Dinner			
Food	**# Servings**	**Fat**	**Sodium**
_____	_____	_____	_____
_____	_____	_____	_____
_____	_____	_____	_____
_____	_____	_____	_____
_____	_____	_____	_____
_____	_____	_____	_____
_____	_____	_____	_____
	Total:	_____	_____

Weather Browser

Subject Area: Geography, Math, Science

Opening Comments

The Interactive Weather Browser, courtesy of Michigan State University, offers countless overlapping activities in geography, math, and science. Some possible activities are listed below to get you started, or you can come up with your own. Page 172 is meant to keep your students thinking throughout their weather browsing session.

Helpful Internet Site(s)

http://www.teachercreated.com/books/3804

Click on page 171, sites 1, 2

Math Activities

1. Find the southernmost negative temperature.
2. Find the northernmost positive temperature.
3. Find one city whose current temperature is twice that of another city. List the two cities. Can you make a guess as to why the temperatures are so different?
4. What is the current temperature difference between New York City and Chicago?
5. What is the mathematical relationship between Celsius readings and Fahrenheit readings?

Science Activities

1. Follow a location's weather over three days, then try and predict its current weather conditions.
2. If the temperature is high, what happens to the humidity?
3. Can you explain why there is such a large temperature difference between two nearby locations? Look for clues in the data you are given.
4. Try to guess some locations that might have a visibility of greater than 15 miles.
5. Find a station that has the same temperature as the one nearest your own city and compare the other readings.

Geography Activities

1. Find the weather station nearest you.
2. Find a weather station with a temperature of more than_____degrees and a humidity of less than_____%.
3. Compare readings of weather stations at similar latitudes.
4. Compare readings of weather stations at similar longitudes.
5. Find a weather station at or near:
    - the midpoint of the Mississippi River
    - the nation's capital
    - the western shore of Lake Erie
    - the Great Salt Lake

Things to Consider

- Use these activities as either the introduction or culmination to a unit.
- Have a weather expert visit your class to talk about what they do and then answer questions.

Weather Browser (cont.)

Name:_____

1. After working with the Interactive Weather Browser, I have two questions about weather.

   a. _____

   _____

   b. _____

   _____

2. If I were a mathematician, I would be most interested in_____

   because _____

   _____

3. If I were a meteorologist, I would be most interested in _____

   because _____

   _____

4. If I were a geographer, I would be most interested in _____

   because _____

   _____

5. Here are two questions I would like to ask other students.

   a. _____

   _____

   b. _____

   _____

 # Scientists' Gazette

Opening Comments

Schools are working hard to breathe more life into science instruction. Here is an activity that could breathe some life into science experiments, especially into follow-up writing that might be required of your students.

Helpful Internet Site(s)

http://www.teachercreated.com/books/3804

Click on page 173, sites 1, 2, 3

Setting the Stage

- When your students decide what science experiments they will perform, they can start searching the Web, FTP sites, and Gopherspace for comprehensible background information on their subjects.

- Review with your students the various sections/features of a newspaper.

- Review with your students the sample provided on page 174.

Procedure

1. Keep comprehensible information that adds to the background of your topic and can then be translated into short newspaper articles.

2. Do a rough draft of your layout so you can envision where information and graphics will go.

3. Copy and paste valuable online graphics from Web pages only after hotlisting the site for easy return and asking permission from that Web site. (What is an effective newspaper layout without pertinent pictures?)

Things to Consider

- For headlines, use the results of your experiment.

- One possibility for articles is to break down each step of the scientific method (problem, hypothesis, experimentation, observation, conclusion) into separate articles.

- Another possibility is to write about the difficulties you may have had in performing your experiment. Put it in dramatic terms, "Harris Nearly Bows Out of Project."

- Think of an original name for your newspaper.

- For commentary, use a student's opinion on a related issue.

- Draw a cartoon that relates to the topic.

Garfield School's Science Times
BLANEY MINIATURIZES WATER CYCLE!

How can humans observe the water cycle in the comfort of their own homes?

Dr. James Blaney and trusty assistant Jason Jackson teamed up to create a water cycle in a cup. The researchers needed sources of heat (a kitchen stove) and cold (ice cubes), a clear plastic container, and, of course, water.

Researchers Encounter H2O Cycle Difficulties

Scientific pioneers Dr. James Blaney and Jason Jackson had their early hopes dampened when observers accidentally spilled the water specimens in the condensation stage of the groundbreaking experiment. But two days later, the scientists were back on track.

"Finally," said water expert Jason Jackson, "We are making progress." After onlookers knocked over the much discussed instant water cycle experiment, Jackson and Blaney reorganized and completed the activity.

"We're lucky we still had ice cubes, or we never would have finished," said Blaney.

The heat of the sun causes water to evaporate or turn into gas.

As the water vapor rises, it reaches colder air, attaches to microscopic dust particles, and condenses into clouds.

When the clouds become oversaturated (too full), they release their moisture. We call that precipitation.

Water Experts Release Findings

At a press conference at Garfield School, the dynamic scientific team of Dr. James Blaney and Jason Jackson announced the results of their on-again, off-again indoor study of the water cycle.

"We are pleased to share our discovery that students everywhere can see the water cycle up close and personal," said Blaney.

"As soon as we poured the hot water into the plastic cup and covered it with plastic wrap, we witnessed the evaporation. Not long after that, we placed the ice cubes on top of the wrap and waited exactly 24.2 seconds before we saw the first droplet form on what you might call the ceiling of our miniature water laboratory. Finally, we witnessed droplets so large that they eventually released water back into the water source at the bottom of the cup."

"Within a span of 2:59 minutes, we observed all three stages of the water cycle," noted Jackson.

 # Going Buggy!

Opening Comments:

Most children love to find out about the bugs and insects in their world. Use the lessons on the following pages in a number of different ways to share information about this intriguing part of our lives. Students find information online and then move offline to finish their worksheets. These pages could be completed as homework, cooperative lessons, in stations, or as a whole class.

Some Helpful Internet Sites:

http://www.teachercreated.com/books/3804

Click on page 175, sites 1, 2, 3, 4

Setting the Stage:

- Complete the Insect Know, Want to Know, Learned (KWL) chart as a class.
- Make bookmarks of sites to visit or put the URLs on cards at the computer.
- Discuss the differences between bugs and insects and review basic insect anatomy.
- Put up word charts/posters to review the vocabulary.
- Have insect reference books and picture books available for student work time.

Procedure:

- Review the worksheets and directions with the students.
- Give students time to browse the sites.
- While online, students look for insects, pictures of the metamorphic stages, and information to add to the KWL chart completed as a class.
- For the metamorphosis page, have students draw the different stages of metamorphosis.
- On the collection sheet, have students find a set amount of insects before filling in the information.
- Students complete their collection sheets and Metamorphosis worksheets.

Special Considerations and Other Options:

- As an option, have students draw and label insects and bugs to use as posters in the room.
- Students could use other materials for the metamorphosis worksheet. When glued onto this page, poppy seeds, macaroni, and cottonballs work well as eggs, larva, and cocoon.

Going Buggy! *(cont.)*

Name:_____

Insects and Bugs Collection Sheet

Kind	Description (What does it look like?)	Insect or Bug	Comments

 # Going Buggy! *(cont.)*

Name:_____

Insects and Bugs K-W-L Chart

What do you know?	What do you want to know?	What did you learn?

Going Buggy! *(cont.)*

Name:_____

Insects and Bugs Metamorphosis

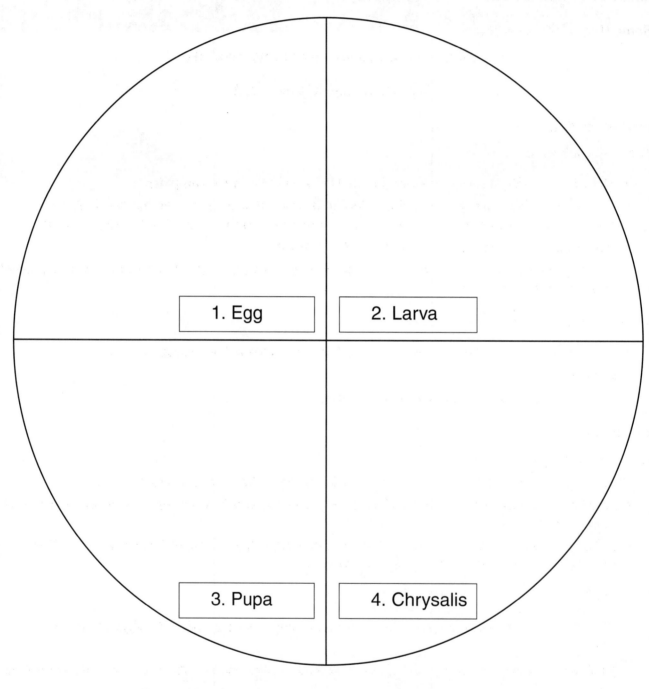

| 1. Egg | 2. Larva |

| 3. Pupa | 4. Chrysalis |

Draw the four main stages of metamorphosis.

Love That Lava

Opening Comments:

Combine earth science, geography, and geology in this exploration of the world's volcanes. There are two lessons in this section. The first has students asking questions of volcanologists. In the second, students map the locations of major volcanos. It may be difficult to move on once your students find all the stimulating activities waiting for them at Volcano World. Just go with the flow.

Some Helpful Internet Sites:

http://www.teachercreated.com/books/3804

Click on page 179, sites 1, 2

Setting the Stage:

Ask a Volcanologist:

- Make bookmarks of sites to visit or put the URLs on cards at the computer.
- Complete a KWL chart with the class. Assign or have students decide on the questions to be asked before going online. Students write their question on the "Ask a Volcanologist" page.
- Define terms. Possibly put up a poster with definitions.
- You may want to have children make a volcano logbook with a glossary and space to take notes of information found online.

World Volcano Map:

- Make bookmarks of sites to visit or put the URLs on cards at the computer.
- Copy the world map on page 181.
- Review the map and instructions with students.

Procedure:

Ask a Volcanologist:

- Children visit one of the Web sites above and find the section about asking questions.
- Students determine if their question has already been answered. If so, write down the response to share with the class.
- If the question has not been answered by an expert at the site, then e-mail the question. When an answer is posted, share the response with the class.

World Volcano Map:

- Students browse through volcano sites to find the geographic locations of volcanoes around the world.
- Students mark their world maps to show locations. Volcano names are written in spaces below the map.
- Another option is to have students label their volcano maps with the longitude and latitude of the volcano locations. (This information is available at the Volcano World site).

 Love That Lava *(cont.)*

Special Considerations and Other Options:

- Students could go to Volcano World and read the stories about *Rocky the Volcano Creature* by Jean Kurtz.
- Have children illustrate a scene from one of Ms. Kurtz's stories. Make a classroom display of the text along with student illustrations. Another option is to have students send their pictures to the Web master for inclusion in the story.
- Take your students on a current-event tour of volcanic activity in Volcano World's volcanic activity database. This source is frequently updated and includes satellite images of current eruptions.

Ask a Volcanologist

1. Write your volcano question on the lines below.
2. Go to a volcano Web site and find the section about asking questions.
3. Look for your question.
4. If it has already been answered, write the answer on the lines below.
5. If your question has not been answered, send your question to the experts. Once you get an answer, write it on your form and share the information with the class.

My Question: _____

_____

_____

_____

The Expert's Answer: _____

_____

_____

_____

 # Love That Lava *(cont.)*

Name:_____

1. Go to a Web site and find the location of several volcanoes.
2. On the map, write a different number for each volcano you find.
3. Write the volcano names in the lines below the map. Make sure each volcano name matches the number you wrote on the map.

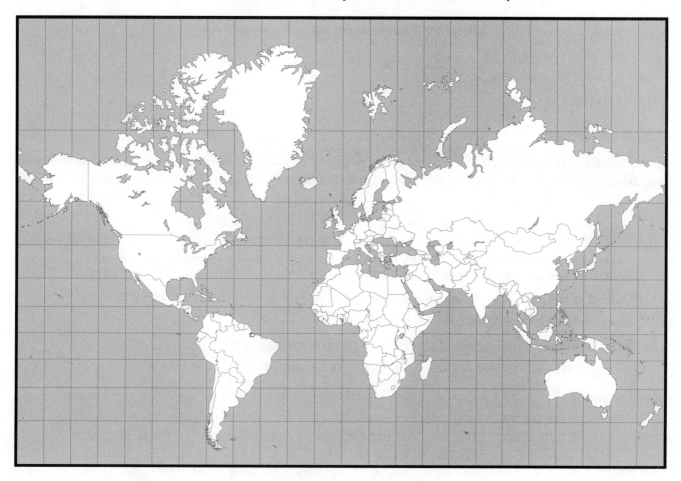

1._____   2._____

3._____   4._____

5._____   6._____

7._____   8._____

 # Rain Forest Stations

Opening Comments:

Stations can be an enjoyable, hands-on method of passing along information. The activities on the following pages are a follow-up after students have discussed the rain forest and visited several Web sites. Students have booklets to complete as they move around the room. These booklets can be sent home or saved for display at Open House.

Some Helpful Internet Sites

http://www.teachercreated.com/books/3804

Click on page 182, sites 1, 2, 3, 4, 5

The Activities

What's That Smell?

In this activity, students smell an item and then try to identify what it is. They then choose the picture that matches their guess and glue it into their station booklet.

Preparation:

1. Visit some of the suggested Internet sites to find a list of rain forest products that are available to you. (suggestions: cinnamon, vanilla, nutmeg, pineapple, banana, coffee beans, coconut, grapefruit, cloves, chili pepper, chocolate, ginger)
2. Collect some small, closed containers (film canisters work very well). Label them A–F.
3. Place an item to be identified in each container.
4. Copy the instruction pages and put them on cards at each station.
5. Copy the pictures (if you decide to use them) for students to put in their booklets.

Mystery Items

In this activity, students reach into an enclosed container (a sock in a cup), try to identify the item inside, and then choose the picture that matches their guess and glue it into their station booklet.

Preparation:

1. Copy the instruction pages and put them on cards at each station.
2. Visit some of the suggested Internet sites to find a list of rain forest products that are available to you. (suggestions: sesame seeds, peanuts, avocado, pineapple, banana, balsa wood, gum (chicle), rubber, jute (rope, twine), coffee beans, coconut, vanilla bean)
3. Place small plastic cups into several socks. These will be the "guessing containers." Label them A–F.
4. Place an item to be identified in each of the cups.
5. Copy the pictures (if you decide to use them) for students to put in their booklets.

Who Lives in the Rain Forest?

At this station, students draw their own idea of what the rain forest looks like.

Preparation:

1. Cut blank paper to match the size of the booklet.
2. Have many colors available to students for the drawing. If possible, use a variety of media as well. Let students use chalk, paint, pastels, markers, crayons. . . whatever you have on hand.
3. Have pictures and books about the rain forest at the station for students to look through.

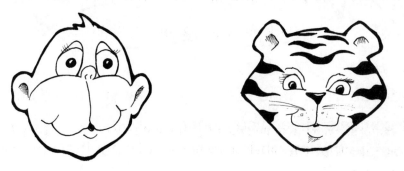

Tour a Rain Forest

This station is best run by an adult or older student who can guide the group on a virtual tour of a rain forest. Students will take a tour and list forest inhabitants in their booklets.

Preparation:

1. Long before deciding to use this station, visit some of the suggested Internet sites and find a park to tour.
2. Copy the instruction page and put it on a card at the station.
3. Set up the class computer with the browser pointed at the site chosen in step one.
4. In the small group, students click through the rain forest.
5. As they tour, students put the names of plants, animals, insects, and other rain forest inhabitants into their booklets.

Create an Insect

After reminding students of an insect's basic anatomy (three body parts and six legs), let your class loose to create their own species of insect. Add these creations to a class rain forest.

Preparation:

1. Copy the instruction page and put it on a card at the station.
2. Copy the "Insect Body Shapes" for each student.
3. Make patterns of the body shapes on oaktag so the students can trace the shapes they want.
4. Have construction paper, glue, and scissors available.

Name:_____

What's That Smell?

1. Visit some Web sites. Find some items that you could smell at school.

2. Smell the contents of each container.

3. Find the picture that matches the smell and put it in your book under the correct letter.

Mystery Items?

1. Visit some Web sites. Find some items that you might be able to touch at school.

2. Place your hand in the cups.

3. Without looking, try to guess what is in them.

4. Place the picture that shows the item under the matching letter.

 # Rain Forest Stations *(cont.)*

Name:_____

What's That Smell?

Smell the contents of each container. Place the picture that shows the smell under the matching letter.

A	B	C	D	E	F

What's That Smell?

Smell the contents of each container. Place the picture that shows the smell under the matching letter.

A	B	C	D	E	F

Rain Forest Stations *(cont.)*

Name:_____

Mystery Items?

Place your hand in the cups. Without looking, try to guess what is in them. Place the picture that shows the item under the matching letter.

A	B	C	D	E	F

Mystery Items?

Place your hand in the cups. Without looking, try to guess what is in them. Place the picture that shows the item under the matching letter.

A	B	C	D	E	F

Rain Forest Stations (cont.)

What's That Smell?

cinnamon	lemon	vanilla	pineapple
cloves	nutmeg	ginger	black pepper
chocolate	coconut	tea	coffee

Mystery Items?

chewing gum	chopsticks	peanuts	chocolate
potato	rubber eraser	banana	wicker basket
yam	teabag	rubber ball	balloons

Name:_____

Create an Insect

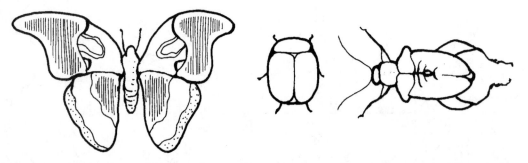

1. Visit a Web site to view insects. Notice the special shapes that make insects.
2. Pick the shapes you want to make your insect.
3. Trace and cut the shapes out of colored paper.
4. Glue the insect together and give it a name.

Tour a Rain Forest

1. Use the Internet to take a tour of a rain forest.
2. As you move through the Web site, put the names of the animals, insects, plants, and other creatures that you see into your booklet.

Rain Forest Stations (cont.)

Name:_____

Tour a Rain Forest

Animals	Plants	Insects	Others

ocelot	kapok tree	toucan	macadamia nuts
jaguar	emerald tree boa	harpy eagle	mango
elephant	poison arrow frog	morpho butterfly	banana
bromeliad	three-toed sloth	cacao	rubber tree

Tour a Rain Forest

Animals	Plants	Insects	Others

ocelot	kapok tree	toucan	macadamia nuts
jaguar	emerald tree boa	harpy eagle	mango
elephant	poison arrow frog	morpho butterfly	banana
bromeliad	three-toed sloth	cacao	rubber tree

Math

What's Cooking?

The Solar System

Size is Relative

The National Debt

Flags of the Sea

How Big is a Whale?

Penny for Your Thoughts

Finding Your Way

We're Goin' Shoppin'

What's Cooking?

Opening Comments:

Children love to cook. What better way can there be to introduce students to fractions, measurement, chemical reactions, direction following, and the many other concepts cooking entails? Send your class today to explore the kitchens on the World Wide Web.

Some Helpful Internet Sites:

http://www.teachercreated.com/books/3804

Click on page 191, sites 1, 2, 3, 4, 5, 6

Setting the Stage:

- Make bookmarks of sites to visit or put the URLs on cards at the computer.
- Have students find out the nation(s) of their family ancestry and choose a recipe from that nation. For instance, since my family's roots are in so many countries, my sons usually choose Germany as a place to study.
- Make a copy of the "Recipe Card" form for each student.
- Review the instructions with the class.

Procedure:

- Students are assigned (or decide on) a recipe type to retrieve.
- Students visit a site and choose a recipe.
- Students write their recipes on the "Recipe Card" form or print it out.

Special Considerations and Other Options:

- Divide students into teams. Have them research recipes by topic: holiday, pasta, Italian recipes, party food, desserts, whatever topic you wish.
- Have a class feast. Students prepare and bring in dishes they discovered online.
- Cook some of the recipes in class.
- Tie this lesson into a cultural study. Food is a super way to introduce children to another country, other traditions, or diverse cultures.
- Bind holiday recipes together into a class book.
- Students rewrite recipes in their own words.
- Collect all the recipes, make a copy for each student, and then make a cookbook for each student. With a personalized cover, this would make a nice Mother's Day gift.

✎ ✎ ✎ What's Cooking? *(cont.)* ✎ ✎ ✎

Name:_____

Recipe Card

Name_____   Serves_____

Recipe_____

Ingredients: _____

_____

_____

_____

Instructions: _____

_____

_____

_____

_____

_____

_____

⬛ ⬛ ⬛ ⬛The Solar System⬛ ⬛ ⬛ ⬛

Teacher Notes

NCTM Standards, Grades 5–8: Problem Solving, Number Relationships, Computation, Estimation, and Measurement.

Objectives:

Students will…

- use the Internet to gather data about the physical and orbital properties of the planets in the solar system.
- make metric unit conversions and make conversions between metric units and customary units.
- convert between scientific notation and standard notation and vice versa.
- construct tables and graphs.
- draw conclusions and make predictions based on their data.
- construct a mathematically accurate model of the solar system.

Materials Needed:

- Computer with Internet access
- Scientific or graphing calculator
- Metric ruler or meterstick
- Poster paper

Web Sites:

http://www.teachercreated.com/books/3804

Click on page 193, sites 1, 2, 3, 4, 5

Keywords for Search Engines:

Using your favorite search engine (such as Google.com)use the names of the planets as keywords.

Time: approximately 3–4 hours

Teaching the Lesson:

- Students will need a review on scientific notation concepts and how to enter numbers in scientific notation into their calculators.
- Before the students complete the physical and orbital data tables, demonstrate how to perform the conversions for one planet.
- If students are having trouble scaling down planet size, suggest a centimeter scale of 1:1 billion.
- Students will discover that the planet distances for a 1:1 billion cm scale model will not fit on a piece of poster paper. Help them experiment with different distance scales so that they can fit the solar system on their papers.
- When students are exploring the relationship between distance from the sun and period, they will need to draw a scatter plot. Since the distances and periods vary so greatly, have students draw the four closest planets to the sun on one plot and the other five planets on a separate plot.

⚐ ⚐ ⚐ ⚐The Solar System⚐ ⚐ ⚐ ⚐

Student Activity Sheet

Name: _____

Date: _____ Per: _____

Andy, the wannabe astronomer, needs your help in constructing a scale model drawing of the solar system. Complete the following steps to show him how it is done.

Physical Data

Complete the following table of physical data of the planets. Locate the data at one of these suggested Web sites or use your favorite search engine to find another site about planets.

Table One: Physical Data of the Planets

Planet	Radius (km)	Radius (miles)	Radius (in scientific notation—cm)	Diameter (km)

Name:_____

Orbital Data

Complete the table below for orbital data.

Table Two: Orbital Data for the Planets

Planet	Distance from Sun (km)	Distance from Sun (miles)	Distance from Sun (in scientific notation—cm)	Period (days)	Period (years)

Scale Models

With the data you collected, help Andy make a scale model drawing of the solar system.

☑ ☑ ☑ The Solar System (cont.) ☑ ☑ ☑

Name:_____

1. First, you have to decide on your conversion factor. Ask yourself what factor you need to reduce the data by so that it will fit on poster board. Experiment with some different values for scales now.

_____

_____

_____

_____

_____

If you are still having trouble, see your teacher for some suggestions. After you have chosen your conversion factor, fill in the table below to help scale down your data before you draw your solar system.

Table Three: Conversion Table

Planet	Actual Diameter (km)	Scale_____ Size in cm	Actual Distance from the sun (km)	Scale_____ Distance in cm

The Solar System *(cont.)*

2. After completing your table, what suggestions do you have for Andy so that he can make his scale model of the solar system fit onto a piece of poster paper?

_____

_____

3. After you have calculated the dimensions for your drawing, construct an accurate model on poster paper. Be sure to label each planet and indicate the scales you are using for size and distance.

Further Explorations

1. After completing his table and making his scale drawing (with your expert help), Andy was feeling pretty good about his chances of becoming an astronomer. In fact, he was sure he would be the one to discover a planet past Pluto. In order to help him narrow his search, he needs to know about how far from the sun the planet would be and what its approximate period would be. Construct two scatter plots that show the period versus distance and make a prediction of the distance and period of Andy's planet. Use the first scatter plot for the four planets closest to the sun. Use the second scatter plot for the next five planets.

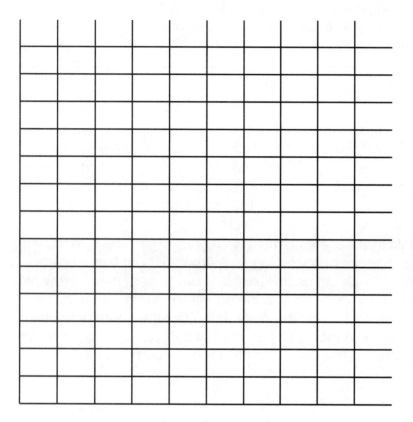

2. Describe the relationship between the distance and the period.

_____

_____

_____

3. If a 10th planet was discovered past Pluto, how far from the sun would it be? What would you expect its period to be? Explain.

_____

_____

_____

_____

Size is Relative

Teacher Notes

NCTM Standards, Grades 5–8: Problem Solving, Reasoning, Connections, Number Relationships, Computation, Estimation, and Measurement.

Objectives:

Students will…

- measure their heights and covert them to feet, centimeters, and meters.
- use the Internet to find the heights of the Washington Monument, the highest point in their state, and the depth of the Marianas Trench.
- set up proportions comparing their heights to the heights of the Washington Monument, the highest point in their state, and the depth of the Marianas Trench.
- calculate the decimal, fraction, and percent equivalents for each ratio.
- make a scale drawing that will include themselves, the Washington Monument, the highest point in their state, and the Marianas Trench.

Materials Needed:

- Computer with Internet access
- Calculators

- Tape measure
- Rulers or metersticks

- Poster paper

Web Sites:

http://www.teachercreated.com/books/3804

Click on page 199, sites 1, 2, 3, 4, 5, 6

Time: approximately 2–3 hours

Teaching the Lesson:

- Have students record their heights in feet by using decimals. You may need to demonstrate how to convert from fractions to decimals.
- The Washington Monument is a suggested comparison. If there is a more familiar landmark or building in your city, then use it.
- Some students will recognize the pattern that is developing in the tables; if they do not, ask questions to lead students in that direction.
- Students will need to experiment with scales for their drawings. Remind them that they will be including other objects that might be much taller or deeper.
- Some students may choose to use the depth of the Marianas Trench as a negative number.

Selected Answers:

- Washington Monument: 555 feet high
- Marianas Trench: 11,020 meters deep

▨ ▨ ▨ ▨ Size is Relative ▨ ▨ ▨ ▨

Student Activity Sheet

Name: _____

Date: _____ Per: _____

Have you ever stood at the bottom of a very tall building and wondered just how tall it was? Think for a moment about the tallest building or the highest mountain you have ever seen. Sometimes it is hard to relate to their massive heights. By comparing a known height, for instance, to how tall you are, you will be better able to understand the relationship between heights of different objects.

How Tall Are You?

A good place to begin your understanding of the height of something is to measure your own height. Work in pairs to measure your heights. Record your height below. Then list your height in inches, feet, centimeters, and meters. For a conversion table go online.

Your height in inches: _____

Your height in feet (use decimals): _____

Your height in centimeters: _____

Your height in meters (use decimals): _____

Washington Monument

Let's see how you compare to the Washington Monument. Go online to find out the height of the Washington Monument. List its height in inches, feet, centimeters, and meters.

Washington Monument height in inches:_____

Washington Monument height in feet:_____

Washington Monument height in centimeters: _____

Washington Monument height in meters: _____

Size is Relative (cont.)

Name:_____

How Do You Stack Up?

1. Compare your height to the Washington Monument's height by setting up a ratio in inches, feet, centimeters, and meters. Express your answers as fractions, decimals, and percents. Fill in the table with your values.

Inches	Fraction	Decimal	Percent
Your Height ⎯⎯⎯⎯ Washington Monument			

Feet	Fraction	Decimal	Percent
Your Height ⎯⎯⎯⎯ Washington Monument			

Centimeters	Fraction	Decimal	Percent
Your Height ⎯⎯⎯⎯ Washington Monument			

Meters	Fraction	Decimal	Percent
Your Height ⎯⎯⎯⎯ Washington Monument			

2. What conclusions or observations can you make about your height in comparison to the height of the Washington Monument. Explain.

_____

_____

_____

Scale Drawing

On a piece of poster paper, make a scale drawing of your height and the height of the Washington Monument. Leave enough room for two more scale drawings.

The High Point of the Lesson

1. Now let's see how you compare to the highest point in your state. Visit a Web site to find the highest point in your state. Record its height in inches, feet, centimeters, and meters.

The highest point in my state is_____

Inches	Fraction	Decimal	Percent
Your Height			
Highest Point			

2. Before you complete the rest of the ratios in the table, make a prediction about what they will be. Explain.

_____

_____

_____

Name:_____

Now complete the rest of the tables.

Feet	Fraction	Decimal	Percent
Your Height / Highest Point			

Centimeters	Fraction	Decimal	Percent
Your Height / Highest Point			

Meters	Fraction	Decimal	Percent
Your Height / Highest Point			

3. Add your state's highest point to your scale drawing. Leave room for one more addition to the drawing.

Size is Relative *(cont.)*

How Deep Is It?

1. This time you are going to compare heights with the deepest point in the world. Where do you think the deepest point in the world is located? For those of you who guessed under water, you're right. In fact, the name of the deepest spot on earth is the Marianas Trench. Go online to find out the depth of the Marianas Trench.

   Marianas Trench depth in inches: _____

   Marianas Trench depth in feet: _____

   Marianas Trench depth in centimeters: _____

   Marianas Trench depth in meters: _____

2. If you were going to fill up the Marianas Trench with duplicates of the Washington Monument, how many monuments would you need to stack on top of each other? Explain.

   _____

   _____

   _____

   _____

3. What is the ratio of the highest point in your state to the Marianas Trench? Also include the decimal and percent equivalents.

   _____

   _____

   _____

   _____

4. Explain how you would estimate how many people standing head to toe would be needed to fill up the Marianas Trench.

   _____

   _____

   _____

   _____

5. Complete your scale drawing by adding to it the Marianas Trench. Look back over your drawing and add any additional information such as scales, labels, or legends.

◪ ◪ ◪ ◪ The National Debt ◪ ◪ ◪ ◪

Teacher Notes

NCTM Standards, Grades 5–8: Problem Solving, Communication, Reasoning, Connections, Number Relationships, and Computation.

Objectives:

Students will...

- use the Internet to record the current amount of the national debt.

- use the national debt to explore number concepts.

- use the Internet to find out the current U.S. population and then use that information to calculate each person's share of the debt.

- use the Internet to access the national debt amount at different times and then use that information to calculate the percentage of increase for the debt.

- calculate the amount required to be paid each month in order to pay off the debt by the time they graduate from high school.

Materials Needed:

- Computer with Internet access

- Calculator

Web Sites:

http://www.teachercreated.com/books/3804

Click on page 205, sites 1, 2, 3

Time: approximately 2 hours

Teaching the Lesson:

- This lesson can be used in conjunction with a lesson on budgeting or with a social studies unit exploring the United States government.

- This lesson can also serve as an extension to a lesson on place value and reading and writing numbers.

- The last section of the activity sheet that deals with paying off the debt may present some difficulties for students. To simplify the questions for students, you can assume that the debt will not increase over the payoff period. Of course, the debt is still increasing, but taking this factor into consideration makes this a very difficult problem.

- Review or introduce the concepts of expanded notation and scientific notation.

✎ ✎ ✎ The National Debt (cont.) ✎ ✎ ✎

Student Activity Sheet

Name: _____

Date: _____ Per: _____

What comes after a billion? Some of you might have answered a billion one, or some of you may have said one trillion. Both answers could be correct, but did you know that one possible answer could have been the national debt? That is right; the national debt is well over one billion. Find out more about the national debt by completing the investigation below.

The National Debt

Go online to find out more about the national debt.

Define what the national debt represents: _____

_____

_____

_____

_____

_____

_____

1. Record the date and time you visited the National Debt Clock site. _____

   _____

2. Record the amount of the national debt. _____

3. Which digit is in the ten billions' place? _____

4. Which digit is in the hundred millions' place? _____

5. Use words to write out the amount of the national debt.

_____

_____

_____

6. Write the amount of the national debt using expanded notation.

_____

_____

_____

7. Write the national debt using scientific notation. _____

Your Fair Share

The national debt is a lot of money. How much does that mean every person in the United States would have to contribute to pay off the debt? Visit the "U.S. Census Pop Clock" online and record the current population estimate.

1. Record the current U.S. population. _____

2. Based on the national debt amount and the U.S. population, how much is each person's share?

_____

_____

3. What is the class's share of the national debt?

_____

4. What is the share of the national debt in the state where you live?

Go online to research and your state's population and record the number below.

State Population: _____

My state's share of the national debt: _____

Just How Big Is It Getting?

1. Visit the National Debt Clock each day for the next two days. Record the date and time and amount of the national debt in the table below (the first line should be the amount from your first visit to the debt clock).

2. Calculate the time that has elapsed between each visit in minutes as well as the change in the debt balance.

Date, Time, and Amounts of the National Debt

Date	Time	Time Difference	Debt Amount	Debt Amount Difference

⚡ ⚡ ⚡ The National Debt *(cont.)* ⚡ ⚡ ⚡

3. Look over your table and calculate the percentage increase of the national debt for each time you visited the debt clock.

   The national debt percentage of increase for each period:

   _____

   _____

   _____

4. Calculate an overall average increase per minute.

   _____

   _____

   _____

Paying Off the Debt

1. Based on the average rate of increase, what will the national debt be when you graduate from high school?

   _____

   _____

   _____

   _____

2. If you were the only one paying, how much would you have to pay each month in order to pay off the national debt by the time you graduate from high school?

   _____

   _____

   _____

   _____

   _____

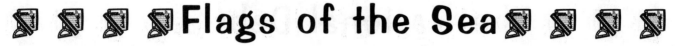# Flags of the Sea

Teacher Notes

NCTM Standards, Grades 5–8: Problem Solving, Communication, Reasoning, Connections, Number Relationships, Computation, Estimation, Patterns, Probability, Geometry, and Measurement.

Objectives:

Students will…

- use the Internet to investigate the mathematics that can be found in International Marine Signal Flags.

- describe signal flags in equivalent terms using fractions, decimals, and percentages.

- conduct a probability experiment using signal flags.

Materials Needed:

- Computer with Internet access and printer

- Calculator

- Poster paper

- Markers

- Rulers, tape measures

Web Sites:

http://www.teachercreated.com/books/3804

Click on page 210, sites 1, 2

Time: approximately 1–2 hours.

Teaching the Lesson:

- Prior to introducing the lesson, encourage your students to pay attention to the flags they see around them and to think of any connections the flags might have to mathematics.

- If you have access to a color printer, it might be useful to print the International Marine Signal Flags. Otherwise, you can print them out and label the different parts of the flags with the appropriate colors.

⊠ ⊠ ⊠ ⊠ Flags of the Sea⊠ ⊠ ⊠ ⊠

Student Activity Sheet

Name: _____

Date: _____ Per: _____

There are flags everywhere you go. You see them in front of buildings, at stadiums, in classrooms, on ships, in parades, and many other places. Flags are important symbols of identification and means of communication. But why do flags look the way they do? In fact, who decides what a flag looks like? And what role do you think mathematics has played in the design of flags?

International Marine Signal Flags

International Marine Signal Flags are a special set of flags used by ships to communicate with each other. Each flag represents a letter which has a special meaning that sends a message to another ship. Take a look at these flags online and then answer the questions that follow.

1. Examine the signal flags carefully and note the key similarities and differences. Pay particular attention to patterns, similarities, and the arrangement of colors.

For instance, you might describe "H" Hotel and "K" Kilo as similar because they both are divided in half by their colors.

Now you try. _____

_____

_____

_____

_____

_____

_____

_____

_____

_____

_____

2. Look at the flags again and try to find all the geometric figures they contain. Name at least four figures. List the figures you found and the name of the flag where you found that figure.

_____

_____

_____

3. What is the most common geometric figure you found in the flags?

_____

4. Look at the flag for "N" November and count the total number of squares it contains. How many squares did you find? In the space below make a drawing that shows all the squares you found.

Fractions and Flags

1. The flag for "E" Echo could be described using fractions. For instance, Echo is $1/2$ blue and $1/2$ red. Look through the flags and describe the five flags found in the table on the next page in terms of fractions.

2. In the remainder of the table, compare sets of flags using fractions. For instance, the blue portion of "G" Golf ($1/6 + 1/6 + 1/6 = 3/6 = 1/2$) is equal to the red portion of "H" hotel, $1/2$.

Flags of the Sea (cont.)

Name:_____

Fraction Tables

Flag Name	Fractional Description:
(Ex.) "E" Echo	½ red and ½ blue
1. "D" Delta	
2. "T" Tango	
3. "U" Uniform	
4. "Z" Zulu	
5. "C" Charlie	

Sets of Flags to Compare	Flag Comparison:
(Ex.) "G" Golf and "H" Hotel	The blue portion of Golf $= \frac{1}{6} + \frac{1}{6} + \frac{1}{6} = \frac{3}{6} = \frac{1}{2}$ or one-half of the total flag which is equal to the red portion of Hotel or ½ of the total flag.
Set 1. "C" Charlie and "D" Delta	
Set 2 "L" Lima and "O" Oscar	
Set 3. "T" Tango and "J" Juliett	
Set 4. "Z" Zulu and "E" Echo	

Name:_____

Flags: Decimals and Percents

Using the information from your previous fraction tables, complete the tables below by converting the fractional descriptions into decimal and percent equivalents. For example, Echo is ½ blue and ½ red; as a decimal it is 0.5 blue and 0.5 red; as a percent Echo is 50% blue and 50% red.

Flag Name	Decimal Equivalent	Percentage Equivalent
(Ex.) "E" Echo	0.5 blue and 0.5 red	50% blue and 50% red
1. "D" Delta		
2. "T" Tango		
3. "U" Uniform		
4. "Z" Zulu		
5. "C" Charlie		

Sets of Flags to Compare	Flag Comparison (using decimals and percentages):
Set 1. "C" Charlie and "D" Delta	
Set 2. "L" Lima and "O" Oscar	
Set 3. "T" Tango and "J" Juliett	

Name:_____

More Flag Questions

1. Print out a copy of the "I" India flag. In that flag, what is the ratio of the area of the black circle to the area of the entire flag?

   _____

   _____

   _____

2. What is the area of the yellow portion of the "I" India flag?

   _____

   _____

   _____

3. Print out a copy of the "S" Sierra flag. What is the ratio of the area of the inner blue rectangle to the area of the outside white rectangle? Draw a diagram to support your answer.

   _____

More Flag Questions *(cont.)*

4. Imagine you could enlarge each flag to the size of a bulletin board and put it on a wall. If you were to throw ten darts, how many times would you expect to hit

the orange in the "O" Oscar flag? Explain.

_____

_____

_____

the blue in the "N" November flag? Explain.

_____

_____

_____

the orange in the "Y" Yankee flag? Explain.

_____

_____

_____

▨ ▨ ▨ How Big is a Whale? ▨ ▨ ▨

Teacher Notes

NCTM Standards, Grades 5–8: Problem Solving, Communication, Reasoning, Connections, Number Relationships, Computation, Estimation, Statistics, Geometry, and Measurement.

Objectives:

Students will…

- use the Internet to make comparisons regarding the sizes of whales.
- investigate the differences in length, weight, area, volume, and speed.
- convert between imperial and metric units.
- write questions based on the information they gather.
- invent a method to measure the volume of a whale.
- use information from the Internet to calculate the time it takes for gray whales to migrate from the Arctic Ocean to Baja California.

Materials Needed:

- Computer with Internet access
- Rope or string
- Centimeter grid paper
- Calculator
- Tape measure

Web Sites:

http://www.teachercreated.com/books/3804

Click on page 217, sites 1, 2, 3, 4, 5

Time: approximately 2–3 hours

Teaching the Lesson:

- You may choose to show a short video or provide some information about whales before introducing the lesson.
- Reinforce the idea of making a comparison to a known object to help in making an estimation of very large objects.
- There are numerous Web sites dealing with whales. You may wish to explore alternate sites.
- If there are enough students in the class, you can go outside and have them stand fingertip to fingertip to demonstrate the arm span calculation.
- For the arm span exercise, break students into groups of four or five.

⬛ ⬛ ⬛How Big is a Whale? *(cont.)*⬛ ⬛ ⬛

Teacher Notes *(cont.)*

- Since whale "heights" are not given, you may need to give additional guidance in transferring the scale drawings to the centimeter grid paper.

- Prior to the lesson, introduce a method to find the volume of an irregularly shaped object.

- Review concepts of area and volume.

Selected Answers:

Whales	Whale Lengths (feet/meters)	Whale Weights (pounds/kilos)
Blue	70/21.3	142,000/64,408
Killer	25/7.6	10,000/4,535
Gray	48/14.6	60,000/27,215

▨ ▨ ▨How Big is A Whale? *(cont.)* ▨ ▨ ▨

Student Activity Sheet

Name: _____

Date: _____ Per: _____

Spend a few minutes thinking about a whale. When you thought of its size, what did you take into consideration—length, width, weight, or maybe something completely different? Sizes can be compared in a number of different ways, but the one thing in common is that all the comparisons rely on mathematics. This investigation about whales will show you how measurements such as length and weight can be used to make size comparisons.

Length

1. Blue, gray, and killer are the names of three common types of whales. Now think about an object that you are more familiar with, let's say a pickup truck. Do you think those whales are longer or shorter than a pickup truck? Explain.

   _____

   _____

   _____

2. Go online and find out how long each type of whale is when it is fully grown. Then fill in the table below with each measurement. Complete the table by making the necessary conversions. Use a conversion table Web site to check your calculations.

Whale Lengths

Whales	Feet	Yards	Centimeters	Meters
Blue whale				
Gray whale				
Killer whale				

3. Visit Web sites to find out the lengths of the pickup trucks. Then list the lengths in the table below.

Pickup Truck Lengths

Pickup Truck	Feet	Yards	Centimeters	Meters
Ford				
Chevrolet				

4. How many pickup trucks would you need to line up bumper to bumper to match the length of a blue whale?

_____

_____

_____

5. How many times longer is a blue whale than a gray whale?

_____

_____

_____

How Big is a Whale? *(cont.)*

6. In a group, measure the length of each other's arm span in inches. Calculate the group's average arm span length. Then answer the following question. How many students with their arms extended end to end would it take to equal the length of one blue whale?

Arm Span Measurements (inches)

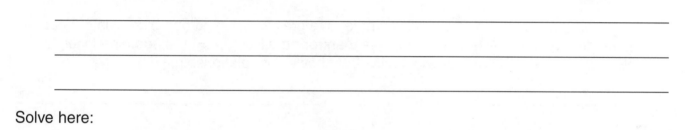

	1.	2.	3.	4.	5.
Arm Span					

Group's average arm span: _____

Number of students to equal one blue whale: _____

7. Write a question that asks about the length of a whale versus another object, person, or animal. Then give your question to another student and have him or her answer it.

_____

_____

_____

Solve here:

8. Using a piece of string or rope, mark off the length of each type of whale. Experiment to find out how many times you can connect the string or rope across the classroom.

Weight

1. Visit the Web sites you used previously and list the weights for blue, gray, and killer whales in the table below.

How Big is a Whale? (cont.)

Whale Weights

Whales	Weight (pounds)	Weight (tons)	Weight (grams)	Weight (kilograms)
Blue whale				
Gray whale				
Killer whale				

2. Is the weight of three gray whales greater than, less than, or equal to (>,<,=) the weight of one blue whale? Write an inequality that shows this relationship.

_____

_____

_____

3. If you added the weight of one killer whale, one gray whale, and one blue whale together, would that amount be greater than, less than, or equal to (>,<,=) the combined weights of 10 gray whales? Write an inequality that shows this relationship.

_____

_____

_____

4. Write a question that uses the weights of the different whales to make a comparison. Give it to another student to answer.

_____

_____

_____

Solve here:

◨ ◨ ◨ How Big is a Whale? *(cont.)* ◨ ◨ ◨

Area

1. Imagine for a moment a whale as a two-dimensional object lying flat on a piece of paper. How could you find the area of that whale? Explain what your procedure would be.

_____

_____

_____

_____

2. Using a piece of centimeter grid paper, make a scale drawing of each type of whale and then calculate its area. List your answers in the table below.

Whale's Area

Whales	Area (inches)	Area (feet)	Area (centimeters)	Area (meters)
Blue whale				
Gray whale				
Killer whale				

3. Measure the area of the floor of your classroom.

Area of Classroom

	Area (inches)	Area (feet)	Area (centimeters)	Area (meters)
Classroom				

⧅ ⧅ ⧅How Big is a Whale? *(cont.)* ⧅ ⧅ ⧅

4. How many classroom floors would it take to equal the area of each type of whale?

Blue:_____

Gray: _____

Killer: _____

Volume

1. Suppose you wanted to compare the volumes of the whales. What procedures would you use to try to calculate their volume?

_____

_____

_____

2. Compare your method for finding the volume of a whale with another classmate's and make suggestions that would improve your procedures.

3. Select one of the whales and calculate its volume using the procedure you developed. Then compare your answer with the anwers of the other students who performed the calculation for the same type of whale.

Speed

1. Go to the Web site for the gray whales and find out how fast they swim.

gray whale speed: _____ mph   gray whale speed: _____ k/h

▨ ▨ ▨ How Big is a Whale? *(cont.)* ▨ ▨ ▨

2. Each year gray whales migrate from the Arctic Circle to Baja California. Use the gray whale Web site and find out how far they travel each year. Then calculate how long (time) the journey takes.

To calculate the time, use the formula time (t) = distance (d) ÷ speed (s) or **t = d ÷ s**.

Distance from Arctic circle to Baja California: _____ miles _____ km

Time

	Hours	Days	Months
Time			

3. Go back to the Web site for the gray whale and find out its life span. What percentage of a gray whale's life is spent migrating back and forth between the Arctic Circle and Baja California?

_____

_____

_____

_____

▧ ▧ ▧ ▧ Penny for Your Thoughts ▧ ▧ ▧

Teacher Notes

NCTM Standards, Grades 5–8: Problem Solving, Reasoning, Connections, Number Relationships, Computation, Statistics, Geometry, and Measurement.

Objectives:

Students will…

- measure the diameter of several different types of coins and use the information to calculate area and circumference.
- use the Internet to find the actual diameter of each type of coin and determine the level of accuracy of their measurements.
- weigh each type of coin and make conversions between metric and imperial units.
- use the Internet to find the actual weight of each type of coin.
- measure the height of each type of coin and use that information to solve problems.

Materials Needed:

- Computer with Internet access
- Calculator
- Gram scale
- Ruler or caliper

Web Sites:

http://www.teachercreated.com/books/3804

Click on page 226, sites 1, 2, 3, 4

Time: approximately 2 hours

Teaching the Lesson:

- You can borrow the scales and possibly the calipers from science teachers at the school.
- When students are measuring the diameter using a ruler, they may have difficulty obtaining a level of accuracy to hundredths of an inch. It is recommended that you have them use calipers instead.
- Errors may result in measuring the diameter because students may be measuring chords instead of diameters. This is a good opportunity to introduce or review the concept of chords and diameters.
- Stress accuracy when students are weighing the coins. If small enough weights are not available, weigh several of the same type of coin at once.

Teacher Notes

Selected Answers:

Coin	Diameter (inches)	Weight (grams)
Penny	0.750	2.5
Nickel	0.835	5
Dime	0.705	2.268
Quarter	0.955	5.67

Penny for Your Thoughts *(cont.)*

Student Activity Sheet

Name: _____

Date: _____ Per: _____

Coins are pretty amazing. Think about it; you give someone a round piece of metal, and they give you stuff. In other words, coins have value. But they only have value if they meet stringent measurements. Learn more about coin specifications by completing the investigation below.

Area of a Coin

Use a ruler or caliper to measure the diameter of a penny, nickel, dime, and quarter to the nearest hundredth of an inch. Calculate the area of one side of each coin and its circumference. Fill in the table with your results.

Area = $\prod \bullet r^2$ Circumference = $2 \bullet \prod \bullet r$ **or** $d \bullet \prod$

let $\prod = 22/7$

Area and Circumference of Coins in Inches

Coin	Diameter (in.)	Radius (in.)	Area (sq. in.)	Circumference (in.)
Penny				
Nickel				
Dime				
Quarter				

1. Write an equation that shows the mathematical relationship between the diameter and the radius of each coin.

_____

_____

2. For each type of coin, what is the ratio of the circumference to the diameter?

_____

3. What did you discover about the ratios in problem number two?

_____

_____

_____

How Accurate Are Your Measurements?

Verify the level of precision you obtained with your measurements by visiting a Web site below and recording the exact specifications for the diameter of each type of coin in the table.

Coin Specifications Comparison

Coin	Actual Diameter (in.)	Measured Diameter (in.)	Difference (in.)
Penny			
Nickel			
Dime			
Quarter			

Were your measurements accurate? Explain.

_____

_____

_____

Penny for Your Thoughts (cont.)

A Weighty Issue

Use a scale to measure the weight of each type of coin to the nearest hundredth of a gram. Record the weight in grams. Then convert the weight to kilograms, ounces, and pounds and record those weights in the table below. To help you in making the conversions, visit a conversion Web site.

Coin Weights

Coin	Grams	Kilograms	Ounces	Pounds
Penny				
Nickel				
Dime				
Quarter				

1. You know that the monetary value of two dimes and a nickel equals a quarter. But what about their weights? Is the weight of two dimes and a nickel greater than, less than, or equal to (>, <, =) the weight of a quarter? Write an inequality describing your answer.

_____

_____

_____

2. How much money would 25 kilograms of nickels equal?

_____

_____

Penny for Your Thoughts *(cont.)*

3. How many pounds of quarters would it take to buy your favorite car? Go online find out how much your favorite car costs.

Price, make, and model of your favorite car: _____

_____

Calculate here:

_____ pounds of quarters are needed to buy my car.

Visit one of the coin Web sites and record the actual weights for each coin.

Coin Weights Comparison

Coin	Measured Weight (g)	Actual Weight (g)	Difference
Penny			
Nickel			
Dime			
Quarter			

☒ ☒ Penny for Your Thoughts *(cont.)* ☒ ☒

4. When you measured the different types of coins, which coin had the largest measurement error?

_____

_____

_____

5. Explain how you might have weighed the coins to obtain a greater degree of accuracy.

_____

_____

_____

Height

Measure the height (to the nearest hundredth of an inch) of each coin and record the results in the table.

Coin Heights

Coin	Penny	Nickel	Dime	Quarter
Height (in.)				

1. How high would 100 dollars in dimes be?

_____

_____

2. What would your height be worth in quarters?

_____

_____

Maps And Map Making

Working with maps extends from the earliest civilizations to the present day. The United States Geological Service has produced a wonderful set of instructional materials on using maps and map-making for students in grades K–12. Some examples from these materials have been included in this book. The principles that underlie the use of maps can be incorporated into various social studies topics including history, geography, anthropology, and archaeology.

The Egyptians, Greeks, and Romans made maps from clay and papyrus. In general, Greek astronomers are credited with inventing latitude and longitude and identifying the location of the Equator. Even though we do not have examples of true maps from before 600 B.C., a great deal of experimentation and knowledge about maps and map-making preceded their actual development. The earliest precursor of a map that has been documented was found in the Ukraine and dates back to approximately 6200 B.C. It is a pictorial representation which has elements that can be identified as related to map-making.

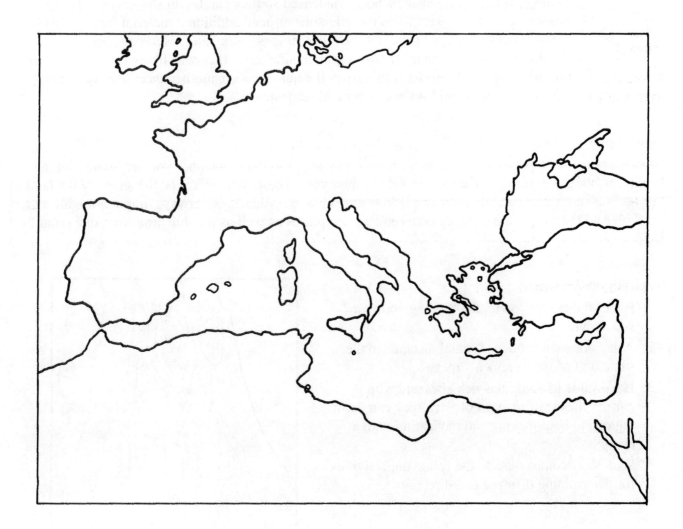

⬔ ⬔ ⬔ Finding Your Way (cont.) ⬔ ⬔ ⬔

Introduce your students to terminology and concepts involved in using maps and a compass to find particular locations.

Materials: compass
Activity Sheet MAP-1: *Tools for Working with Maps*

Web Site:

http://www.teachercreated.com/books/3804

Click on page 234, site 1

Keywords for Search Engines:

Using your favorite search engine (such as **Google.com**), use keywords "map" and "compass."

Preparation: Since these lessons are adaptations of some lessons presented by the United States Geological Service, they have been condensed so they can be finished over a shorter time-period. If you wish to do more lessons or need additional material for a particular lesson, visit the site and print out the other lessons. Ask students to pay special attention to any vocabulary terms they encounter since they will likely be used in other lessons. They will also need to answer the questions on another sheet of paper. This will serve as a record for the teacher and student.

Topographic Maps

A topographic map tells you where things are and how to get to them, whether you are hiking, biking, hunting, fishing, or just interested in the world around you. These maps describe the shape of the land. They define and locate natural and man-made features like woodlands, waterways, important buildings, and bridges. They show the distance between any two places as well as the direction from one point to another.

Teaching the Lesson:

1. Have students log on to the "finding your way" site above.

2. Ask students what does "actual distance in the same unit of measurement" mean?

3. Have students study the web sites and with a partner make suggestions of what they can do in regards to map-making and navigating with a compass.

4. With their compasses, do the following activities for determining distance and direction.

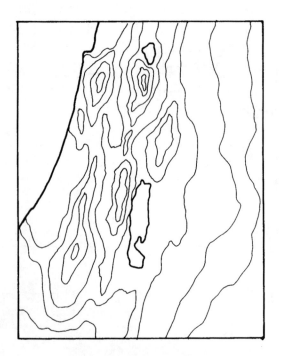

▧ ▧ ▧ Finding Your Way (cont.) ▧ ▧ ▧

Measuring Distances

Distance is measured between points on the map by aligning the scale with "0" on one point and extending the scale bar toward the other point. If these points are close enough to each other, you can read the number of feet or miles between them on the scale. If they are too far apart for that, put a strip of plain paper down on your map, and mark the strip where it touches the two points. Then match this marked strip with the appropriate scale printed in the margin of the map and figure the distance from a series of comparisons with the scale. Read the distance on a curving road or fence line the same way. Mark a strip of plain paper at the ends of relatively straight stretches of road or fence, and then compare the marked strip with the scale.

Determining Direction

To determine the direction, or bearing, from one point to another, you need a compass as well as a map. Most compasses are marked with the four cardinal points—north, east, south, and west—but some are marked additionally with the number of degrees in a circle (360°: north is 0° or 360°; east is 90°, south is 180°, and west is 270°.) Both kinds are easy to use with a little practice.

1. Take a compass bearing from a map:

   - Draw a straight line on the map passing through your location and your destination and extending across any one of the map borders.

   - Center the compass where your drawn line intersects the map border. Align the compass axis N-S or E-W with the border line and read on the compass circle the true bearing of your drawn line. Be careful to get the bearing in the correct sense because a straight line will have two values 180° apart. Remember north is 0°, east is 90°, etc.

   - To use this bearing, you must compensate for magnetic declination. If the MN (Magnetic North) arrow on the map magnetic declination diagram is to the right of the true north line, subtract the MN value. If the arrow is to the left of the line, add the value.

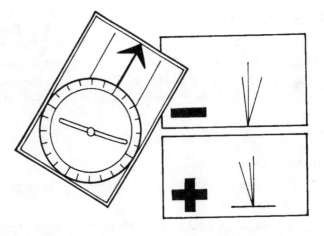

🖎 🖎 🖎Finding Your Way *(cont.)* 🖎 🖎 🖎

Extended Activity #1:

If you wish, you can also have students create their own maps by going to one of the sites shown below:

http://www.teachercreated.com/books/3804

Click on page 236, sites 1, 2, 3

Extended Activity #2

1. In preparation for making their maps using information gathered from the students' reading of the map-making materials, have students make a list of the decisions they will need to make regarding:

   - type of map
   - ratio (scale)
   - size of map
   - area covered by map

Working with Maps

Name:_____

Directions: In the space below, draw a map of your school and its grounds. Use the information you learned online to help you. Use a compass to help you determine direction.

◪ ◪ ◪We're Goin' Shoppin'◪ ◪ ◪

Subject Area: Math

Objective
Students practice using decimals, working with larger numbers, and budgeting as they take a virtual shopping trip.

http://www.teachercreated.com/books/3804

Click on page 238, sites 1, 2, 3, 4

Setting the Stage
- Review with your students place value in all the tens, hundreds, and thousands places.
- Assign word problems that require addition, subtraction, and even multiplication of money, especially in the thousands columns.
- If you want your students to use a calculator, practice strategies for calculating money amounts.

Procedure
1. When you feel your students are mathematically prepared to shop, announce to them that you have just given them $_____ (fill in own amount) that they are to spend on the World Wide Web.

2. Review the following project guidelines:
   - — minimum number of purchases
   - — use of calculator
   - — inclusion or exclusion of sales tax
   - — clearly defined reasons for the purchase

3. Review the product page with your students and tailor it to their needs.
4. Let them shop.

Things to Consider
- Review the purchases.
- Review the math with calculators.
- Review the Web sites and shopping strategies that were most helpful.
- Discuss what they would have done with another $1,000.

Shopping Expense Summary

Name of shopper: _____

Total expenditure allowed: _____

Minimum number of purchases allowed:_____

Purchase #

Item description: _____

Gift recipient: _____

Reason for selection: _____

Price: _____

Tax (if applicable): _____

Web site used: _____

Total spent: _____

Purchase #

Item description: _____

Gift recipient: _____

Reason for selection: _____

Price: _____

Tax (if applicable): _____

Web site used: _____

Total spent: _____

Purchase #

Item description: _____

Gift recipient: _____

Reason for selection: _____

Price: _____

Tax (if applicable): _____

Web site used: _____

Total spent: _____

Art

Online Museum Tour

Origami Originals

At the Circus

Online Museum Tour

Opening Comments:

There are museums of all types around the globe. Unfortunately, most of us cannot get to many of these wonderful treasure houses. Good thing that more and more museums are going online.

Have your students visit several sites online. After everyone has done their research, have students share their information with the class in the form of an online guide to the world's museums.

Some Helpful Internet Sites:

http://www.teachercreated.com/books/3804

Click on page 241, sites 1, 2, 3, 4, 5, 6, 7, 8

Setting the Stage:

- Visit a few museum sites and become more familiar with who is online.
- Discuss the idea of an online museum with your students. See the Art Museum Tourist Log for points to bring up.
- Review the Tourist Log with the class and set a deadline.

Procedure:

- Have students complete the offline portion of the Art Museum Tourist Log before going to the Internet sites.
- Give students time to browse the sites.
- After completing their forms, students will make a final draft of their information.

Special Considerations:

- Depending on the ability level of your class, you may want to begin this project by assigning a student or group of students to find and copy a listing of online museums. This may make it easier to divide up the museums between students.
- After collating the Tourist Logs, you may want to leave a copy of the book in the classroom, a copy in the school library, and send a copy to the local public library.

✎ ✎ Online Museum Tour (cont.) ✎ ✎

Name:_____

Art Museum Tourist Log

Complete the offline questions on this worksheet before moving to your chosen museums.

1. What is an online museum? _____

   _____

2. What do you think you will find at the sites you visit? (check all that apply)

   ❏ Audio clips   ❏ Video clips   ❏ Text information   ❏ Graphics

   ❏ Images of artwork   ❏ Photography   ❏ Modern art   ❏ Folk art

   ❏ Sculpture   ❏ Furniture   ❏ Scientific equipment   ❏ Paintings

   ❏ Cultural recordings   ❏ Historical artwork   ❏ o Other

3. What might an "interactive" museum site have that another museum may not?

   _____

   _____

Now go to the web and see what you can find!

1. Museum and URL: _____

2. Where is this museum located?_____

3. When was the museum established? _____

4. Type of museum: _____

5. After visiting the museum online, use a different color pen. Recheck the boxes above to show what you actually found at the web site.

Art Museum Tourist Log (cont.)

6. Type(s) of artwork at this site: _____

_____

7. Are there private collections housed at this museum? If so, list two collections along with the names of the donors and the type of artwork donated.

_____

_____

_____

8. Is this an interactive site? If so, what details about the site make it interactive?

_____

_____

9. Tell three things that you liked best about this museum.

   • _____

   • _____

   • _____

10. Would you recommend that someone else visit here? Why or why not?

_____

_____

_____

Origami Originals

Opening Comments:

The ability to create a box, plane, hat, or even a kangaroo from paper has fascinated children of all ages for many years. The ancient art of Japanese paper folding, origami, is a enjoyable, habit-forming method of teaching the geometry of basic shapes and angles to elementary school students.

Some Helpful Internet Sites:

http://www.teachercreated.com/books/3804

Click on page 244, sites 1, 2, 3, 4, 5

Setting the Stage:

- Make bookmarks of sites to visit that have models or put the URLs on cards at the computer.
- Cut lightweight paper into 6" (15 cm) squares or purchase origami folding paper.
- Practice basic folds with the class.
- Begin with the simple model level as some origami folding can get quite difficult.
- Perhaps train a couple of students as origami masters so they can troubleshoot any folding difficulties the class may have.

Procedure:

Step 1: Folding

- Students visit some Web sites and decide on a shape to create.
- Using the models at their site, students fold an origami creation.
- Students may print the models or fold their creations while online.

Step 2: Browsing Through the Galleries

- Several of the sites mentioned above have "galleries" of photographs showing origami creations.
- Before or after making their creations, students browse through the Origami sites and list something found there. This information can then be recorded on the "Origami Originals Worksheet" on page 51.

Special Considerations and Other Options:

- You may want to make a poster that demonstrates and labels a few of the basic folds.
- Another possibility is to have students visit an assigned site to create a certain model.
- Use this page to tie into a unit on Japan, geometric shapes, or animals.

Origami Originals (cont.)

Name:_____

Origami Originals Worksheet

Site:_____

URL: _____

I found something at this site that I want to share with you. I found_____

_____

_____

_____

_____

- -

Site:_____

URL: _____

I found something at this site that I want to share with you. I found_____

_____

_____

_____

_____

At the Circus

Objective:

The circus can bring out the kid in nearly everyone, both young and old. Students will especially treasure a virtual visit to the world's "Greatest Show on Earth" as they learn about circus performers and unique jargon.

Materials Needed:

- chalkboard
- poster board or chart paper
- 1 copy of page 249 for each student

Focus Web site:

http://www.teachercreated.com/books/3804

Click on page 246, site 1

Alternative Web sites:

http://www.teachercreated.com/books/3804

Click on page 246, sites 2, 3, 4

Keywords for Search Engines:

Using your favorite search engine (such as **Google.com**) use keywords such as "circus," "the big top," and "circus terms."

At the Circus (cont.)

Pre-Internet Activity:

Help students brainstorm a list of what they might see at the circus (e.g., food, animal acts, clowns, trapeze artists, rides, the "Big Top," ringmaster, jugglers, acrobats, etc.). Write them on the chalkboard. Have students share which things are their favorites. Ask about what kinds of acts they might see at a circus. How did the performances make the students feel?

Teaching the Activity:

1. Review the list of circus favorites from the pre-Internet activity. Have the students vote on their favorite part of the circus. Make a bar graph of the results on a sheet of poster board. Display it in the hallway or on a bulletin board entitled "The Greatest Show on Earth."

2. The class will now have a chance to learn more about the circus. Distribute a copy of the activity from page 249. Visit the Web site as a class. Instruct the students to draw one of their favorite circus performances and two acts they learned about on the Internet. Encourage students to use any new vocabulary they have learned.

3. A circus is like a city in and of itself. The members of a circus act as a family. They even have their own language! That is, to the unknowing visitor, they may *seem* to be speaking a different language. Students will enjoy learning some circus jargon at a circus terms website. Write the following puzzles on the board. Challenge pairs of students to discover the terms in "circus talk."

   A movable restroom—D _ _ _ _ _ _
   Common name for an elephant—B _ _ _
   Person who sells popcorn, cotton candy, and other snacks—B _ _ _ _ _ _
   Someone who plays in the circus band—W _ _ _ _ _ _ _ _ _
   Shortened performance—J _ _ _   R _ _ _ _ _ _ _
   Cotton candy—F _ _ _ _
   A new circus performer—F _ _ _ _ of M _ _
   Where the circus performers eat—P _ _ C _ _
   A hard circus worker—R _ _ _ _ _ _ _ _ _

4. For further circus study, read about the lives of circus performers. Have the students compare the life of a circus performer to their own lives. Have the students write an essay explaining the advantages and disadvantages of living with a circus.

Extended Activities:

- Following a unit on the circus, what could be more entertaining than performing in an original circus? As a class, brainstorm all aspects of a circus that make it so entertaining. Students should consider their own talents and skills when creating the list. Then assign tasks for them to undertake that match their talents. Each performer is responsible for his or her own act. Some possible entertainers are these:

Dancer	Hula Hooper
Gymnast	Artist
Juggler	Rope Jumper

Students may also wish to prepare animal acts. They design masks and costumes and choreograph a unique animal act.

One person should act as the Ringmaster. This person surveys his or her classmates' performances and arranges a suitable itinerary of events as well as introductory dialogue. This person may also be in charge of creating a circus bulletin or program and advertising posters.

- Let us not forget that no circus would be complete without the playful antics of clowns. This is the perfect opportunity for the class clowns to play their roles. The following sites offer viewers ideas on what to do and how to act. Clowns should think of original names for themselves and then prepare acts filled with jokes, tricks, and just plain silliness!

http://www.teachercreated.com/books/3804

Click on page 248, sites 1, 2

- If any of the students are interested in juggling, they may visit this site for step-by-step directions to learn this skill.

http://www.teachercreated.com/books/3804

Click on page 248, site 3

- Once the circus stars are ready to perform, arrange a time to visit a younger grade to put on the class' rendition of The Greatest Show on Earth! (Do not forget the peanuts and popcorn!) This show must go on!

Under the Big Top!

Name:_____

Go online to learn about the circus.

Then draw three acts or performers you might see at a circus.

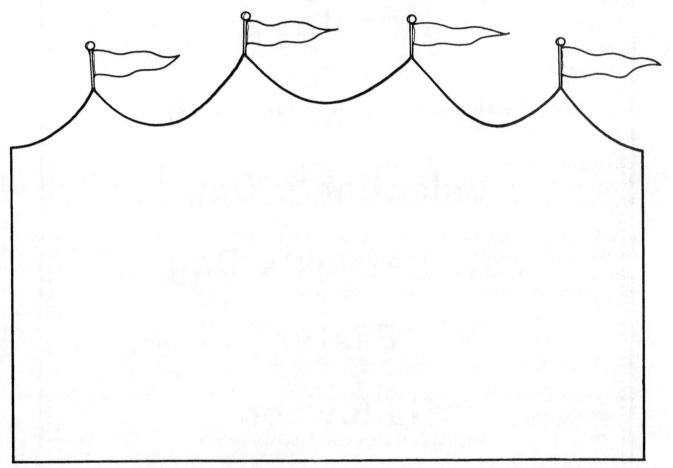

If you were going to be a circus performer, what would you be? Write on the lines below a few sentences describing your life as a circus performer.

_____
_____
_____
_____
_____

Holidays

Chinese New Year

Valentine's Day

St. Patrick's Day

Easter

Halloween

Thanksgiving

Christmas Around the World

 # Chinese New Year

Objective:

Add these Chinese traditions to the New Year. Students record the years that family and friends were born, and then use the Internet to learn the years' animals and characteristics.

Materials Needed:

- chart paper
- chalkboard
- 1 copy of page 254 for each student

Focus Web site:

http://www.teachercreated.com/books/3804

Click on page 251, site 1

Alternative Web sites:

http://www.teachercreated.com/books/3804

Click on page 251, sites 2, 3, 4

The Twelve Animals of the Chinese Zodiac

Rat	Ox	Tiger	Rabbit
Dragon	Snake	Horse	Goat
Monkey	Rooster	Dog	Pig

Pre-Internet Activity:

Lead a discussion about American New Year traditions. Students should understand that our calendar year begins anew every year at 12:01 a.m. on January first. Explain that in China, the calendar year is in the 4000's. Each new year begins on various days, depending on the phases of the moon. The Chinese also assign an animal to each new year. The animals, based on their personalities, determine the kind of year it will be and the personalities of people born under those signs.

Teaching the Lesson:

1. Lead a discussion about what is meant by a personality trait. Have the students brainstorm some traits, and then describe what a person might do to be assigned that trait. Record their responses on a chart.

   Example:

Friendly	Talks to me, invites me to his or her house
Happy	Smiles a lot
Nice	Says nice things to people
Grumpy	Frowns, says mean things

   After the students have listed ten to twenty traits, have them think of two friends or family members and the traits they would assign them.

2. List the twelve animals of the Chinese calendar on the board. (See page 255.) Ask the students to assign these animals personality traits. Which animal do the students think they are most like?

3. Distribute the activity on page 258. Read the directions with the class. Students write their name and the year they were born on the appropriate lines for number one. Then they list the names of two people on the lines for numbers two and three. As homework they must discover the year those people were born and write it under their names. (Remind students that they will need this information to complete the Internet assignment.)

4. Launch the Web site with the class. Show students how to find out their sign(s). The students will need to click this link and then the year they, their family members, or friends were born, one at a time. To demonstrate, click your own birth year (real or imaginary). Read the information about the animal that influences that year. Show the students how to list three traits regarding this animal on their sheets. Demonstrate the use of the **<Back>** arrow from the taskbar to return to the previous page.

5. Try to pair students who have the same years listed on their papers. Allow time for the students to access the site with their partner(s).

6. After everyone has had a chance to gather the information, ask them if the animals' personalities truly reflect the people's personalities. What about this year? Have events in the students' lives reflected the current year's animal traits?

Chinese New Year (cont.)

Extended Activities:

- Have the students think of cartoon characters for as many of the twelve animals as they can and movies or television shows in which the animals starred. List some of the traits of matching animals from the Chinese New Year. Do the cartoon animals and Chinese animals have matching personalities?

- Have the students make a birthday card for someone whose sign they learned about. They should include a picture of the animal that influences their year and a brief description of the animal's traits.

- Have the students make stick puppets of Chinese New Year animals of their choice. Review the animals' traits and write them on cards. Place the puppets and cards at a center for students to use to role-play various situations wherein the puppets reflect the personalities the students read about.

- The Chinese Lantern Festival marks the end of the fourteen-day celebration of the Chinese New Year. Have the students make Chinese lanterns. Students draw and cut designs in 12" x 18" (30 cm x 46 cm) sheets of colorful construction paper. Curve the two short edges so that the edges overlap and glue them in place. Students cut streamers to attach to the bottom of the lantern. Attach strings of yarn to the tops to suspend the lanterns from the ceiling.

  Visit the Web site with the class to learn more about this festival.

  http://www.teachercreated.com/books/3804

  Click on page 253, site 1

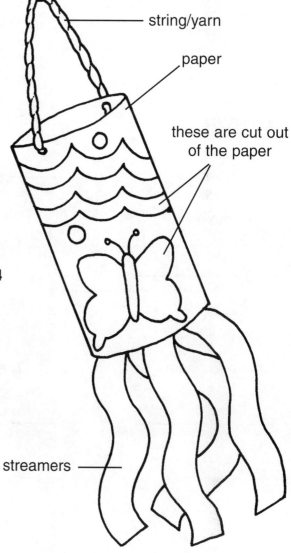

string/yarn

paper

these are cut out of the paper

streamers

Chinese New Year *(cont.)*

Name:_____

Directions: Write your name on the first line. Write your birth year underneath. Write the names and birth years of two family members or friends for whom you wish to discover. Then visit a Web site and find out which animal influences the birth years. Read about the animals and write three personality traits these animals have. Report back to your family and friends and tell them which animals influence their birth years.

1. Your name   The Year of the   Personality Traits

_____   _____   _____

Birth Year   _____

_____   _____

2. Friend's name   The Year of the   Personality Traits

_____   _____   _____

Birth Year   _____

_____   _____

3. Friend's name   The Year of the   Personality Traits

_____   _____   _____

Birth Year   _____

_____   _____

 # Valentine's Day

Objective:

The giving of flowers is a traditional way to show someone we care. Students will fall in love with the Internet as they learn about the meanings of the colors of roses.

Materials Needed:

- chalkboard
- drawing paper
- colored construction paper
- 1 copy of page 258 for each student
- red, yellow, pink, and white construction paper for roses; green for leaves
- white construction paper

Focus Web site:

http://www.teachercreated.com/books/3804

Click on page 255, site 1

Alternative Web sites:

http://www.teachercreated.com/books/3804

Click on page 255, sites 2, 3, 4, 5

Keywords for Search Engines:

Using your favorite search engine (such as **Google.com**) use keywords such as "Valentine's Day" and "rose color meaning."

Valentine's Day (cont.)

Pre-Internet Activity:

Begin a discussion with the class about how people show friendship. Make a list of the students' ideas on the chalkboard. Then ask them to tell things friends should never do. Divide the class in half. Have one half draw a picture and write a sentence telling what friends should do. The second half draws a picture and writes a sentence telling something a friend should not do. Post the students' illustration in the hall under two labels: "Friends Should..." and "Friends Should Not..."

Teaching the Lesson:

1. Write some color words on construction papers matching the color names and post them on the chalkboard. Have the students say the color words and share what images or feelings the colors bring to mind. (Red might remind students of fire or heat, pink for petals on a flower or sweet-smelling bubble gum, etc.)

2. Tell the students that different colors of roses send different messages and feelings. Have them make educated guesses regarding these colors: red, yellow, pink, and white.

3. Distribute a copy of the activity on page 258. As a class or in groups, have the students access the destination URL and find out if their guesses were correct.

4. Have the students use what they learned to make a Valentine card with a bouquet of roses, using the pattern below. They glue the roses on a 9" x 12" (23 cm x 30 cm) sheet of white construction paper, draw and color a vase, and affix green paper leaves. Then they write a "Roses are red" poem, address it, and give it to their Valentine.

5. At this same Web site, read selected topics of interest and learn more about Valentine's Day as a class. Some worthwhile highlights are "Valentine Crafts," "Holiday Food," "Holiday Facts," "Some History," and "Holiday Plants." Try also some valuable "Valentine Links" located at the top of the Web page.

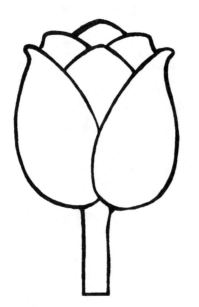

Roses are red,
Daisies are yellow,
You are cute,
And a really nice fellow!

Valentine's Day *(cont.)*

Extended Activities:

- Select one of the holidays crafts or foods listed at this site to make with your students. Love and the Valentine's Day spirit will certainly be in the air!

- Visit one of the alternative sites with the class. Have students take turns reading the information about the history of Valentine's Day. Students write a summary of events from a particular time in history on 6" x 9" (15 cm x 23 cm) note cards. Connect the cards to make a time line of the history of Valentine's Day.

- Another option is to use the information from the alternative Web sites as a sequencing activity. Have pairs of students write a different event in the history of Valentine's Day on sentence strips. Put them in chronological order, and then have volunteers act out the events.

  Print the pictures as they are downloaded, mount them onto construction paper for added durability, and then place them at a center for students to practice sequencing skills.

- If your school has Internet capabilities (an electronic connection within a community), have the students send a Valentine's Day greeting to another teacher. Students practice letter writing skills to compose a kind message, and then e-mail it to a teacher of their choice.

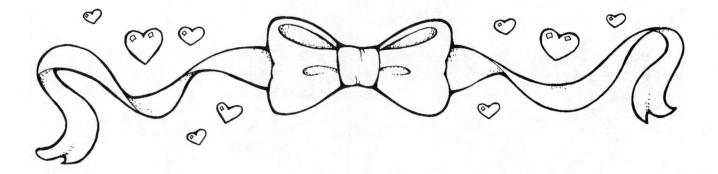

Valentine's Day (cont.)

Name: _____

Directions: Many people give roses or other flowers to show they care. Find out the modern meanings of the different colors of roses. Color these roses to show what you mean.

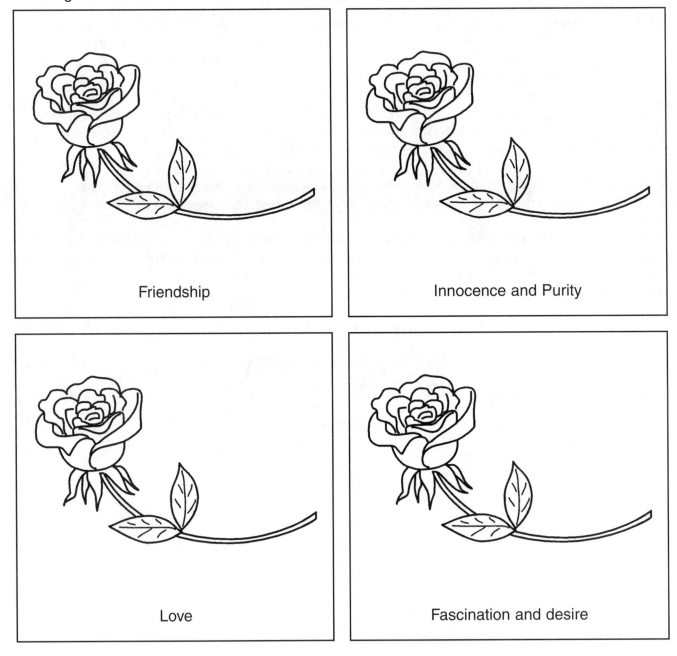

Friendship

Innocence and Purity

Love

Fascination and desire

St. Patrick's Day

Objective:

Bring students the luck o' the Irish as they learn fun-filled facts about everyone's favorite "wear green" day.

Materials Needed:

- green writing or copy paper
- 1 copy of page 262 for each student
- traceable shamrock patterns from page 260
- green construction paper

Focus Web site:

http://www.teachercreated.com/books/3804

Click on page 259, site 1

About this site: Here is a simple yet entertaining site filled with St. Patrick's Day trivia and related terms.

Alternative Web sites:

http://www.teachercreated.com/books/3804

Click on page 259, sites 2, 3, 4, 5

Keywords for Search Engines:

Using your favorite search engine (such as **Google.com**), use keywords such as "St. Patrick's Day" and "leprechaun."

St. Patrick's Day (cont.)

Pre-Internet Activity:

Divide the class into teams of three or four students. Give each group a sheet of green paper and have the groups work together to make a list of "green" objects. Have the groups share their lists with the class. Then ask the students to think about why the color green is representative of St. Patrick's Day. Accept all reasonable responses. Explain that the students will have a chance to visit a Web site to learn how green became associated with this holiday as well as a "wee" bit more information about the holiday and St. Patrick himself.

Teaching the Lesson:

1. Read the information at the Web site about leprechauns. Talk to students about creating "Wanted" posters of leprechauns. Students should include a picture and brief description of the leprechauns, telling why they are wanted.

2. Make patterns of the shamrock below. Have the students trace and cutout three patterns on green construction paper. Then they write a true or false statement about St. Patrick's Day on each clover. (Explain how to reword a true sentence to make it false.) Collect everyone's clovers, and then play "St. Paddy's Day Trivia." Place all the clovers facedown. Select one at a time. Read the sentence. If the students think the sentence is true, they stand up and hop once like a leprechaun. If they think it is false, they remain seated and call out, "Blarney!" Verify any questionable statements at the Internet site.

🎆 🎆 🎆 St. Patrick's Day *(cont.)* 🎆 🎆 🎆

Extended Activities:

- Keep all the true sentences the students wrote from number 3 on page 264. Attach several gold-wrapped Hershey's Kisses to the shamrocks and hide them in the room. (Save the leftover candies.) Give each team of three to four students about two minutes to find a "pot of gold." Once students find a treasure, they must sit down. When their time expires, they must sit down and let the next team take a turn. If all the shamrocks have not been found after everyone has had a turn, allow the least quiet leprechauns to try a second time. Give each student a treat after the game is over.

- Students can send a St. Patrick's Day greeting over the Internet to a friend's (or relative's) e-mail address by following the simple directions at this Web site:

http://www.teachercreated.com/books/3804

Click on page 261, site 1

If students know the e-mail address of a friend or relative, have them bring it to school. (Obtain parental permission for students to e-mail.) Log onto the Web site, and then follow the easy directions to send a card. Students may also include a short message besides the holiday greeting. Students can even send the card to themselves to see what it looks like! The person on the receiving end will have a note on his or her e-mail to log onto the Web site to retrieve the card. They can then enter a series of numerical codes to retrieve the note card.

This is a fantastic way to safely help students experience the benefits of cyberspace!

- Have the students pair up to write an original story about a St. Patrick's Day topic. Remind students of the story elements:

Beginning	Characters, Setting
Middle	Problem
	Events
Ending	Solution

After planning their stories, the students write and illustrate them on green typing paper. Allow time at the end of class for students to share their work with their classmates.

Leprechaun Hunt!

Name:_____

Directions: After reading the online information about leprechauns, imagine that you are hunting one in order to get his pot of gold. You might have read on one of the websites you went to that leprechauns are not social or friendly, so your leprechaun might be hard to find.

In the box below, draw a "Wanted" poster of your leprechaun. Describe him on the lines under your drawing.

Now write about your leprechaun hunt. Did you catch him and get the pot of gold? Or did he get away from you?

_____

_____

_____

_____

Easter

Objective:

Students will "hop" right to learning about the word Easter and the traditions and history behind the holiday.

Materials Needed:

- chalkboard or chart paper
- small piece of paper
- plastic eggs and baskets
- 1 copy of page 266 for each student
- 9" x 12" (23 cm x 30 cm) sheet of construction paper for each student
- small Easter candies

Focus Web site:

http://www.teachercreated.com/books/3804

Click on page 263, site 1

Alternative Web sites:

http://www.teachercreated.com/books/3804

Click on page 263, sites 2, 3

Author's Note: Please keep in mind that Easter, like Christmas, is a religious holiday. Some activities or information at this Web site may be unsuitable for students of certain religions. Be sure to check out the links prior to beginning the activities with the class. Use your best judgment to determine whether the links are appropriate for all your students.

Pre-Internet Activity:

Have the students list animals that are born live and those that hatch from eggs. What will students predict about rabbits and their origins? Ask the students to consider why the Easter bunny and eggs became symbols for Easter if bunnies are born alive. Explain to the students that they will visit a site to answer this question. They will also learn the French, Italian, and German words for Easter.

Teaching the Lesson:

1. Discuss some Easter traditions in the United States. List them on the chalkboard or on a chart. Have the students vote for their favorite custom.

2. Ask the students to write down an Easter wish on a small piece of paper. Have them place it inside a plastic egg. Collect the eggs and place them in a decorative basket. Explain to the students that the Easter Bunny will be by soon to pick up their eggs and listen to their wishes. However, he will only come if students pay close attention at the Web site and answer all the questions on the activity page.

3. Distribute a copy of the worksheet on page 266. Read the directions with the class. Access a Web site as a class. Have students take turns reading the information. (Some words may be difficult for very young learners.) After the class has completed reading the information, work together to complete the activity page.

4. Review the Easter customs and traditions of the countries spotlighted at the Web site. Discuss how Easter celebrations in other countries are alike and different from ours. Have the students illustrate and write a sentence comparing Easter traditions in the U.S. to another country. Students fold a 9" x 12" (23 cm x 30 cm) sheet of construction paper in half. They illustrate and describe United States traditions on one half and those of another country on the other half. Have the students form an egg-shaped circle on the floor and share their work with their classmates.

5. After school, remove the students' Easter wishes and replace them each with a piece of holiday candy. Place one egg on each student's desk for their return the next morning. Explain that the Easter Bunny must have been very proud of their work on the Internet the day before.

Extended Activities:

• The Internet is the place to be to share Easter crafts with the class! The following site offers numerous easy-to-make crafts especially designed for children. Read over the abundance of crafts and select one or two that are the most interesting. Students can either follow the directions from the Web site or follow printed directions.

http://www.teachercreated.com/books/3804

Click on page 265, site 1

• More fun on the Web is awaiting the students. Here you'll find a host of unique Easter-related Internet activities young learners will truly enjoy. Included are cards, coloring pages, egg hunts, clip art, and other Easter links.

http://www.teachercreated.com/books/3804

Click on page 265, site 2

Name:_____

Directions: Read the online information about Easter traditions. Write one tradition in each of the Easter eggs below. Then color the Easter Eggs.

 # Halloween

Objective:

The Internet can be a haunting place for the weak at heart! Teach the classroom goblins and ghouls some Halloween safety tips to ensure everyone a safe trick-or-treat experience.

Materials Needed:

- 1 copy of page 270 for each student

- orange construction paper measuring 9" x 12" (23 cm x 30 cm) for each student

Focus Web site:

http://www.teachercreated.com/books/3804

Click on page 267, site 1

Alternative Web sites:

http://www.teachercreated.com/books/3804

Click on page 267, sites 2, 3, 4

Keywords for Search Engines:

Using your favorite search engine (such as **Google.com**), use keywords such as "Halloween" and "Halloween Safety."

Halloween (cont.)

Pre-Internet Activity:

Ask the class what they like best about trick-or-treating. Have a few students share a successful outing. Then discuss some things that could go wrong (*eating candy that has been tampered with, tripping and falling on the concrete, the bag ripping open, bigger kids wanting to take their candy, etc.*). For each event, have the students brainstorm steps they can take to avoid these troublesome events. Then tell the class that they will learn more safety tips on the Internet so that everyone has a happy time trick-or-treating.

Teaching the Lesson:

1. Distribute a copy of the activity on page 270. Read the directions with the class. You may wish to complete this activity as a class or have the students work in teams of three or four to conduct their own research.

2. Have the students use what they learned on the Internet to make a Halloween safety tips bulletin board. Enlarge the jack o' lantern below. The students cut a 9" x 12" (23 cm x 30 cm) sheet of orange construction paper into a pumpkin shape. Assign the class the task of writing safe things you should do (*walk under a streetlight*) or should not do (*never eat candy unless Mom says it's okay*). Each student writes one safety tip on his or her pumpkin and decorates it to resemble a jack o' lantern. Post the students' artwork on a bulletin board entitled, "Jack's Happy Halloween Tips."

Extended Activities:

- What would Halloween be without the classic scary story? At the site listed below, students can share in a haunting tale. This is just the right amount of frightful fun to make Halloween complete.

http://www.teachercreated.com/books/3804

Click on page 269, site 1

Have the students follow a story outline to create their own haunting tale, "The Legend of (Name of Your School)." Students plan the characters, setting, problem, events, and conclusion, and then write their stories. Turn out the lights and have the students share their spooky tales, a few each day, during oral reading time.

- If the students are more interested in fun and games, they may access this Web site. Students will find pictures to print and color, crafts to make, puzzles to solve, and clip art to view.

http://www.teachercreated.com/books/3804

Click on page 269, site 2

- Challenge the students to take an online Halloween quiz.

http://www.teachercreated.com/books/3804

Click on page 269, site 3

Follow **The Great Halloween Quiz** links to arrive at the first of several Halloween questions.

Halloween Safety Tips

Name:_____

Directions: Read about how to be safe while trick-or-treating. Put an "x" over unsafe acts.
Color the people that are following smart safety rules.

Thanksgiving

Objective:

Turkey, pumpkin pie, mashed potatoes and gravy are the traditional foods served at a modern Thanksgiving table. However, where are the venison, swan, and duck? Students learn about the foods served at the first feast shared between the Pilgrims and Chief Massasoit and his friends.

Materials Needed:

- drawing paper
- chalkboard or chart paper
- 1 copy of page 274 for each student
- 18" x 6" (46 cm x 15 cm) sheet of colored construction paper for each student
- enlarged turkey pattern on page 272 for bulletin board

Focus Web site:

http://www.teachercreated.com/books/3804

Click on page 271, site 1

Alternative Web sites:

http://www.teachercreated.com/books/3804

Click on page 271, sites 2, 3, 4, 5

Keywords for Search Engines:

Using your favorite search engine (such as **Google.com**), use keywords such as "Thanksgiving" and "Thanksgiving traditions."

Thanksgiving (cont.)

Pre-Internet Activity:

Have the students draw and color a typical Thanksgiving table. They should include all their favorite (and not-so-favorite) foods. Have the students share their traditional meals with the class. List the most frequently mentioned foods on the chalkboard or on a chart.

Teaching the Lesson:

1. Discuss why many students' Thanksgiving meals seem to include a number of common dishes. Explain that a *tradition* is an act which becomes regular when several people do it over a long period of time. Turkey, mashed potatoes, and pumpkin pie are all traditional Thanksgiving dishes. Then explain that although this is true now, the very first Thanksgiving meal included quite a number of other foods. Have the students use what they know about the Pilgrims and Native Americans to guess the kinds of foods they served in 1621.

2. Explain to the students that they will have a chance to read about the first Thanksgiving feast on the Internet. Distribute a copy of the activity sheet on page 274 to each student. Read the directions. Have students look at the eight animals featured around the table and guess which they think were probably served.

3. Launch the destination URL with the class. Have students volunteer to read the paragraphs. After reading the information at this site, have the students correctly list the five animals mentioned that were part of the first Thanksgiving meal. Then they color, cut, and paste the pictures on the table.

4. Thanksgiving, although not a national holiday until Abraham Lincoln's proclamation in 1863, is a time set aside to give thanks for all the good fortune in our lives. This was true for the first feast, and now the tradition continues some 350 years later. Review why the Pilgrims wished to show their thanks by hosting the first Thanksgiving feast. Then have the students describe something for which they are thankful. Have each student cut a 6" x 18" (46 cm x 15 cm) sheet of colorful construction paper into the shape of a feather. They write their notion on the feather-shape. Enlarge the turkey pattern on this page. Display the turkey and feathers with the students' thanks on a bulletin board entitled "We Give Thanks."

Extended Activities

- Have the students' parents pitch in to provide a true-to-life Thanksgiving feast just like the first one in 1621. Link to the recipes available from **the Thanksgiving Primer**. Have parents volunteer to prepare one or two of each food. Assign a day and time to feast, and let the festivities begin!

- All people may be thankful for their heritages, and many are somewhat familiar with their family histories. It is true, too, unless a person's family is of Native American descent, everyone's families have immigrated to the United States. Have students and/or parents share what they know about their family histories. Then visit this Web site to read about how other families came to live in the United States.

http://www.teachercreated.com/books/3804

Click on page 273, site 1

Have pairs of students select a person's family history to read on the Internet. They prepare a brief presentation describing about whom they read and how his or her family came to live in America. Use this information to motivate students to learn more about their family's history by discovering from which countries their ancestors originated. Allow one week for the students to gather their information. Enlarge a world map. Place sticky dots (available in the office supply section of your favorite store) with the students' initials on the countries of their ancestors. Discuss the data on the map. Is there any one country that seems popular? Which countries aren't represented at all?

- Satisfy the students' curiosity about the history behind the holiday by reading the original documents that established an "official" day of thanks. All except the *Mayflower Compact* are in their original language. (Surprisingly, they aren't too lengthy.) Students may read the *Mayflower Compact* in both its original form and in modern English. Links also take viewers to the First Thanksgiving Proclamation of 1676, the 1782 Continental Congress, George Washington's Proclamation of 1789, and Abraham Lincoln's of 1863. Select this web site for more learning ideas.

http://www.teachercreated.com/books/3804

Click on page 273, site 2

Food for All

Name: _____

The First Thanksgiving Feast

Directions: Read about the foods the Pilgrims shared at the first Thanksgiving feast. Color and cut out the animal foods on which they and the ninety Native Americans feasted. Paste them on the table.

Christmas Around the World

Objective:

The holiday season brings joy and warmth to everyone. Help students to share in the holiday cheer by learning about some holiday customs from around the world.

Materials Needed:

- a copy of page 278 on chart paper
- 12 copies of page 278, one for each group
- world map
- gold stars or other small stickers
- 12 sheets of 9" x 12" (23 cm x 30 cm) drawing paper, one for each group
- 2 additional sheets of drawing paper

Focus Web site:

http://www.teachercreated.com/books/3804

Click on page 275, site 1

Alternative Web sites:

http://www.teachercreated.com/books/3804

Click on page 275, sites 2, 3

Keywords for Search Engines:

Using your favorite search engine (such as **Google.com**), use keywords "Christmas Around the World" (including quotation marks), or the name of the country being researched and "Christmas."

▨ ▨ Christmas Around the World (cont.) ▨ ▨

Pre-Internet Activity:

During circle time, have the students share their most memorable Christmas traditions. Explain that they will have an opportunity to use the Internet to learn about some holiday customs and traditions from countries around the world. Have them anticipate the types of activities they think will be similar to or different from traditions in the United States.

Teaching the Lesson:

1. Copy the activity sheet from page 278 onto a chart. Fill it in as if the students were studying Christmas traditions in the United States. Demonstrate how to use the information to write a brief summary. Divide the class into up to twelve groups. Make one copy of the activity page for each group. Assign each group a country or region to study by writing in the name of the country or` region at the top of the page (see list below). Then distribute the activity page to the leaders of the teams.

   Asia | Latin America
   Eastern Europe | The Middle East
   France | The Netherlands
   Germany | Scandinavia (Sweden, Norway, and Denmark)
   Greece | Spain
   Italy | The United Kingdom

2. On a world map, show the students where each country or geographic area is located. Mark these locations on the map with a gold star or other identifiable object.

3. Allow time for each group to access the Internet and gather the information to complete the page.

4. Have each team use their information page and summary to make an illustrated book page on a 9" x 12" (23 cm x 30 cm) sheet of drawing paper (or use 12" x 18" (30 cm x 46 cm) paper for a larger book). Collect all the teams' book pages and have the class help organize them in alphabetical order.

5. As a class, decide on a title for the book. Assign one person to make a cover for the book. Include a table of contents page listing all the countries in alphabetical order. Combine the pages to make the resulting book. Share it with the class. Have each team read their summaries and tell about their pictures. Discuss any similarities and differences the students notice among worldwide celebrations of Christmas.

6. Place the book in the library for others to enjoy. Or, allow one person from the class to take the book each night to share with his or her family.

Extended Activities:

- From the focus Web site, take advantage of the information about four other holidays: Hanukkah, Kwanzaa, Ta Chiu, and Yule. Select one holiday to study each day. Access the Web site with the class, read the information, and then discuss any similarities and differences the students observed between Christmas and these holidays.

- Christmas is probably one of the students' most beloved holidays. Challenge their knowledge of the season both here and abroad by taking an online quiz at this Web site.

http://www.teachercreated.com/books/3804

Click on page 277, site 1

Have a student volunteer to keep track of hits and misses by tallying the results on the chalkboard. Start a new tradition by sharing this site with parents at a holiday party. Encourage fun-loving competition between students and parents!

- Your students can see what Santa is up to by dropping in at his home in the North Pole.

http://www.teachercreated.com/books/3804

Click on page 277, site 1

- You may also try accessing the search engine *Yahooligans;* around Christmastime. Chances are the home page will spotlight numerous enticing sites for young learners. Set aside time one day to simply link at random to Christmas sites that interest you. It is guaranteed that the Internet will make your students giddy with excitement about the holiday season.

Christmas in_____

Name:_____

Directions: Learn online about the country listed at the top of the page. Read about how people who live in this country celebrate the holiday season. Fill in as much information as you can on the lines beside each category.

Foods they eat

_____

_____

_____

_____

_____

_____

Decorations they display

_____

_____

_____

_____

_____

_____

Another name for Santa Claus _____

How he arrives _____

What he brings _____

Other holiday traditions_____

_____

_____

_____

Use this information to write a summary about Christmas in the country you are studying. Write the summary on the back of this paper.

Collaborative Projects

Online Book Reviews

Collaborative Projects

Partner Poems

Cyberwriters Needed!

Smarter Than the Average Textbook

Lost: One Entire School

Creating Class Bookmarks

Online Book Reviews

Opening Comments:

Many teachers assign book reports to their class. These written reports are then read and tossed as soon as the student is finished with them. Why not let your students share their thoughts on books they've read with the rest of the Internet community instead?

Some Helpful Internet Sites:

http://www.teachercreated.com/books/3804

Click on page 280, sites 1, 2, 3, 4

Setting the Stage:

- Decide on and post your grading criteria for this project.
- Review book reports in print and online with your students.
- Discuss what makes a good review.
- Post components of a review on charts in the room for easy reference.
- Remind students to intrigue readers without revealing the ending.
- Explain to students that they will be posting their book reports online.

Procedure:

- Make a copy of the directions for submitting book reviews to Book Nook.
- Include directions for other children's writing sites like KidPub.
- Have these instructions available so the students can review them as they work.
- Distribute and discuss copies of the review form on page 285, and begin reading.

Special Considerations:

- Remember that there are many sites that publish children's writing. E-mail the webmaster to see if that site accepts student reviews before suggesting your students send their work.
- Make sure that each child submitting a review has a consent form to allow the release of his or her work online.

Online Book Reviews *(cont.)*

Fill in the information below, then write your book review. Have someone else correct your paper before you send it to a web site. Be sure you have reviewed the submission guidelines for the site where you wish to be published.

Book Title: _____

Author: _____

Publisher and year of copyright: _____

Main characters: _____

_____

_____

Did you enjoy the characters? Why or why not? _____

_____

Where and when does the story take place? _____

_____

Summarize the plot: _____

_____

_____

_____

What did you enjoy most about reading this book? _____

_____

_____

_____

Did you like the ending? Why or why not? _____

_____

_____

_____

Collaborative Projects

Opening Comments:

Your class is studying weather (geography, holiday customs, community history, etc.) and the children want to learn about the same topic from other parts of the world. Pick your topic, then place a call for collaboration. Partner classes from all over the world will help you collect the information your students are looking for.

Helpful Internet Sites:

http://www.teachercreated.com/books/3804

Click on page 282, sites 1, 2, 3

Setting the Stage:

- Pick your topic and set a deadline for responses.

- With your class, brainstorm questions to ask the participating classes.

- Send out the call for collaboration. (See page 284 for an example project.)

Procedure:

- Have students in your class answer the questions they brainstormed.

- Collect data from online participating classes.

- Collate and graph answers to the questions asked.

- Send class results to collaborating classes.

- Make posters to post the results at your school site.

Special Considerations:

- You may want to limit the number of participating classes, depending on your comfort level with collecting and organizing the data.

- Make sure the information is clear in your request for participants. Projects are much easier if everyone really understands the objectives and limitations of the study.

- Try the project out on a small scale with a colleague at your site. This may help work some of the "bugs" out of the project.

Project Design Steps:

1. **Find a topic, question or local issue that you would like to research with your students.**

2. **Identify the learning objectives** (including goal statement and means of assessment) for the project.

3. **Decide how the information will be collected.** Will partner classes be interviewing people in their community? Will the questions be in a survey format?

4. **Establish a time line.** How long will the project last? When will you present it to the Web community? Make sure your project does not interfere with school calendar restrictions.

5. **Break the project down into smaller steps and establish deadlines for these.** This will help you better monitor the progress of the project. For each step, have a list of jobs that need to be completed.

6. **Decide how you will present the information from the project.** Plan for students to make presentations to the staff, parents, school board, and involved community. Make sure there are plans to share the results with those classes that collaborated. Also share your project and the results with other teachers online.

7. **Introduce the project to your school.** Get the site administrator, parents, site councils, PTA, local businesses and the school board involved. This is an important step after the project is flushed out, but before it is initiated.

Decide whether you will introduce the project before or after you have completed the above six tasks. Presenting your project to the people at your site can make your job easier. Let them know what you are doing, why, the time line, when they can get a copy of the results, and most of all, let them know how they can help. The most successful projects are performed with the awareness of the whole school community.

Calling for Collaboration:

To call for collaboration from other interested teachers online register your project with one of the sites listed below. Check these sites for information on project design as well as online forms for registration. Global SchoolNet lists projects chronologically by month of start date and puts them on a matrix for interested parties to review. There are many educational organizations that foster and encourage technology partnerships among teachers.

Educational Organizations:

http://www.teachercreated.com/books/3804

Click on page 283, sites 1, 2, 3

Collaborative Projects (cont.)

Wonderful Snacks—A Global SchoolNet Cooperative Project

Opening Comments:

The Global SchoolNet Foundation is a resource center for educators integrating technology into their curriculum. *Wonderful Snacks* was a project posted with GSN by Carolyn Shandrowski, and reprinted here with permission. This project was designed to help 6th and 7th graders learn to better use spreadsheets, as well as think about the snacks they eat. This project is included as it is posted at GSN as an example of what a collaborative project might look like.

Purpose:

To help my class and others use a spreadsheet effectively. We are interested in finding out what 6–7 graders eat for snacks. Are we any different with what we eat from others in the same grade and throughout the world? To learn from other cultures what they eat at snack time.

Subject:

Multi-disciplinary. This project will help students explore the many uses of spreadsheets. Receiving, analyzing, and communicating with others will be very helpful and practical for them.

Grade Level: 6th and 7th grade

Summary:

We are learning how to use a spreadsheet. We surveyed our class and are learning how to input labels, values, formula, and functions. Our emphasis is on snacks because we believe that middle school aged children eat more than their share of snack-type foods. We want to compare and contrast what type of snacks other students in our grade level eat. A survey will need to be taken of students and results sent to us to analyze. Results will be given back to you.

# of Participants: no limit

Register: October 21–November 4

Send in Project Results: November 25–December 13

Responses back: January 31, if not sooner

Collaborative Projects (cont.)

Name:_____

Project Design

1. **Topic, question, or local issue:**

2. **Learning objectives:**

   Goal Statement:

   Assessment:

3. **Methods:** (how information will be collected, question format, all the project particulars)

4. **Time line:** (Project length, when to present to school and Web communities)

Collaborative Projects *(cont.)*

5. **Deadlines along the way:** (those little jobs that need to be done in order to present the project to the school community, Web community, collect, analyze, and redistribute/report the data)

Date: **Task:**

Date: **Task:**

Date: **Task:**

Date: **Task:**

Date: **Task:**

Date: **Task:**

Project Design (cont.)

6. Presenting the information:

   a. How will the school and Web communities receive the information from your project?

   b. What form will the presentations take?

   c. What materials are needed?

Partner Poems

Subject Area: Language Arts

Opening Comments

Though many teachers have had their students do partner poems before, not many have done so online. For the first time around, let the online partners get a feel for the process, and if they turn out a high-quality poem, so much the better. If you have a second round of writing, challenge the same partners to compose an eight-line poem on another topic with greater emphasis on clarity and coherence, as well as imagery and, if you wish, rhyme.

Helpful Internet Site(s)

http://www.teachercreated.com/books/3804

Click on page 288, sites 1, 2, 3

Setting the Stage

- Call for collaboration. Set a deadline for responses. If your partner poems idea generates considerable interest, here are two things you can do: (1) Send a polite "Thanks, but we are now committed to another school," response. (2) Send a list of respondents to all those expressing interest. With the list, they can connect their own partnerships.

- Once you have your partner class, connect with the teacher and match up your students. How you do this is up to you, but knowing your students' capabilities and interests will help in this process.

- Keep rhyming dictionaries nearby, if needed.

- Decide beforehand, (or let your students decide):
    - the tone of the poem (serious, humorous, totally nonsensical, etc.)
    - the style (rhyming, free verse, etc.)
    - the length (this can always be adjusted)

Procedure

1. To keep e-mail load to a minimum, try to keep the submissions typed into one or two main files.
2. Partner students should send each other an introduction.
3. Set up a template in your word processor so your students can find/submit the latest line to their poems.
4. School A students write/send the first line.
5. School B students write the second line and send back the first two lines.
6. School A students write the third line and send back the first three lines.
7. This continues until completion.
8. Do some partners want to do further revision? If you wish, allow interested partnerships extra e-mail exchanges to polish their work. Keep it manageable, though.
9. Students and teachers team up and edit their poems along the way.
10. Illustrations? Why not have partners create their own versions and exchange copies?

Partner Poems (cont.)

Name: _____

Partner's Name: _____

Title of poem:_____(If necessary, fill it in after the poem is completed.)

Line 1: _____

Line 2: _____

Line 3: _____

Line 4: _____

Line 5: _____

Line 6: _____

Line 7: _____

Line 8: _____

Which lines were mine? _____

Revisions I made during the process: _____

_____

_____

What I liked about my partner's work: _____

_____

_____

What I liked about this process: _____

_____

_____

How I would improve this process:_____

_____

_____

CyberWriters Needed!

Subject Area: Language Arts

Opening Comments

Courtesy of the Texas Education Network, this project was advertised on the KIDSPHERE mailing list in January, 1996. It sounded simple and fun. Ideally, if your timing is right, you will be able to join this specific project, but there is no reason you cannot start your own version. The advertised project called for writers in grades 2–4 but again, if you organize your own, adjust the guidelines and requirements to your liking.

Helpful Internet Site(s)

http://www.teachercreated.com/books/3804

Click on page 290, sites 1, 2

Setting the Stage

- Make a call for collaboration with another class(es).
- Teach/review nouns, verbs, and adjectives.
- Model the basic premise of the activity.
    - Have a student make a list of three nouns, three verbs, and three adjectives.
    - Make believe a student sends it to you.
    - On the overhead/chalkboard, create a story from the word list the student gave you.
    - Make your own list of nouns, verbs, and adjectives.
    - Have the student create his/her own story.
    - It might be helpful to have this model's lists and stories prepared ahead of time.
- Tell your students they will be following the same process with another class.

Procedure

1. Once you are partnered up, e-mail to the teacher the basic format of the activity and the worksheet. Also make sure you know the number of students in your partner class.
2. Have your students make their lists.
3. Double-check the spelling. Make sure the student's name accompanies the list.
4. Accumulate the stories into one text file.
5. Enlist a group of high achievers who are willing to do the word processing, create extra stories or word lists in case your partner class has more students than your class, and fill in for those students who do not follow through on their parts of the project.
6. Exchange the files with your partners.
7. Students write, proofread, and revise their stories.
8. Exchange the stories.

Things to Consider

- Students write positive critiques of partners' stories
- Authors draw pictures to accompany their stories or readers draw/send back pictures to accompany the authors' stories.
- Try another round but this time use different parts of speech or selected phrases.

CyberWriters Needed! (cont.)

Author's name:_____

These words came from _____

Three Nouns	Three Verbs	Three Adjectives
1. _____	1. _____	1. _____
2. _____	2. _____	2. _____
3. _____	3. _____	3. _____

_____

_____

_____

_____

_____

_____

_____

_____

_____

My favorite part of this activity:

_____

_____

I would change this activity by:

_____

_____

_____

Information Sources

Subject Area: Various

Opening Comments

Give your students the opportunity to research a topic on the internet. While your students practice some one-upmanship (on their textbook), they will also be brushing up on their Net research skills. It should also provide more thought-provoking or in-depth information than their textbooks offer.

Place a limit on their research time on the computer for these three reasons.

1. It helps the students concentrate on the activity.
2. It will keep your students on course. A ticking clock might get them to think twice before following the countless links that could land them at the top of the Eiffel Tower when they really want information on the elevation of Death Valley.
3. It allows for more groups to cycle through.

Helpful Internet Site(s)

http://www.teachercreated.com/books/3804
Click on page 292 sites 1, 2, 3, 4, 5, 6, 7, 8, 9, 10

Setting the Stage

- Choose subjects to research.
- Brainstorm with your class some topics related to the chosen subjects.
- Tell your students they have a time limit for their online search. (Give student groups ten minutes on the Net to start with.)

Procedure

1. Groups should have subtopic sheets ready.
2. Start the stopwatch.
3. Repeat this process with other research groups.
4. Those groups waiting to do research could be brainstorming subtopics or watching other students at the computer.
5. The information does not count if it is already in the textbook.

Things to Consider

- Create an insert for the textbook, using your newfound information.
- Using your new information, create a table or spreadsheet.

Information Sources

Name(s): _____

Topic to research: _____

Brainstormed subtopics:

    1. _____

    2. _____

    3. _____

Information sources

Web sites used:

    1. _____

    2. _____

    3. _____

    4. _____

Key facts found: (You may want to attach your copied, pasted, and referenced material.)

The next time I research a topic on the Internet, I will remember:

_____

_____

_____

_____

Feed Me

Lost: One Entire School

Subject Area: Science

Opening Comments

While the Internet is not an actual place, it feels and resembles one. This place is so large that entire institutions of learning might well be lost. This activity offers your students a chance to play detective and get to know other Internet-connected schools at the same time. First, to acquaint your students with the activity, have them play the role of sleuth. After they find one missing school, have them create a similar scenario and put out a call for help.

Helpful Internet Site(s)

http://www.teachercreated.com/books/3804

Click on page 294, site 1

Setting the Stage

- Select a school from the above-mentioned sites.
- Record information about the school that will translate into solid, but not obvious, clues.
- Arrange the clues from general to specific in order.
- Announce the following to your class/group:

  A whole school has been lost on the Internet, and it is your job to find it.

  As is the case with most detectives, you will not be showered with clues. You will pick them up one or two at a time. When you get the clues, you may need to do a little book research and interviewing to check your hunches. It is also each detective's job to complete the clue-by-clue account of your investigation.

Procedure

1. Release the clues one at a time to get the detectives to gradually narrow their search.
2. Your clues might suggest some of the items listed below: (Also, let the lost school's Web site dictate the content and nature of the clues.)
   - Winter climate in the city where the school is located
   - Nickname of the state in which school is located
   - Capital of the state in which school is located
   - One of the school's goals
   - School's enrollment
   - City's claim to fame
3. Let the lost school know that they have been found and returned. They will be relieved.
4. Now that your students have found a school, have them create another lost school scenario and issue a plea for help from other schools. Send the necessary information from these pages to interested classes and begin the search.

Things to Consider

- Offer a credential of completion to any other school which also finds the missing school.
- Pay your kids funny money for efficient research. If they earn a certain dollar amount, let them have a little class celebration.

Lost: One Entire School *(cont.)*

Name:_____

Detective's Diary

Name of detective: _____

Date of disappearance: _____

It is my job to _____

My partners are _____

My informant is _____

Clue # _____

I think that_____

so I:

- went to the Internet and _____
- searched the books and_____
- interviewed _____ to find out _____
  _____
- other

Clue # _____

I think that_____

so I:

- went to the Internet and _____
- searched the books and_____
- interviewed _____ to find out _____
- other _____

Clue # _____

I think that_____

so I:

- went to the Internet and _____
- searched the books and_____
- interviewed _____ to find out _____
  _____
- other _____

Creating Class Bookmarks

Opening Comments:

Bookmarks, or a hotlist, are a group of Web sites that you may want to revisit often. Add the site to your list, and the next time you want to visit, click on the bookmark button. A pulldown menu will appear from which you can select the name of your site. While it may take time for each student to choose a site to add to the class bookmarks, this is good practice in browsing and presenting new information as well as evaluating quality sites. Be sure to set guidelines for student bookmark choices to keep the subject choices within the educational realm.

Helpful Internet Site(s):

http://www.teachercreated.com/books/3804

Click on page 296, sites 1, 2, 3, 4, 5, 6, 7

Setting the Stage:

- Practice making bookmarks
  —When you find a site you will want to revisit later, click on the "bookmark" button.
  —Choose the "Add to Bookmark" option.

- Copy the bookmark instructions on page 297 to place by the computer for student reference.

- Model how to create a bookmark. (Explain that most browsers allow you to edit the name of the selected site for clearer titles.)

- Make a task card with the steps to follow. Put this by the computer for reference.

- Discuss the criteria and deadline for acceptance of a Web site into the class list.

- Discuss student expectations: (1) Add a Web site to the class bookmarks. (2) Be so familiar with the site that you can present it to a group of students or the whole class.

Criteria for Acceptance of a Web Site into the Class Hall of Fame

1. Site fits into the assigned theme (if there is one).

2. Site is fun.

3. Site is educational.

4. Student can clearly state why the Web site is of educational value.

Procedure:

- Students need to review the criteria and look for new/interesting sites.

- Students will complete the worksheet on page 298.

- Students should review the site before making any presentations.

- Students will present their sites to the class (or a chosen group).

Creating Class Bookmarks (cont.)

Special Considerations:

- You could have students choose new bookmarks when a new theme or subject is covered in class. Divide bookmarks alphabetically by theme, by group project, etc.

- Have students share their bookmark information on any mailing lists you participate in.

- Students could publish the best bookmarks, categorized by subject, in school flyers or papers.

- For good public relations and further collaboration, have students inform the chosen site's Web master that the site has qualified for the class bookmarks. (Be sure to include the criteria for selection.)

Make a Bookmark

1. Browse through some Internet sites.

2. When you find a site you want, click the **bookmark** button.

3. Click **add to bookmarks**.

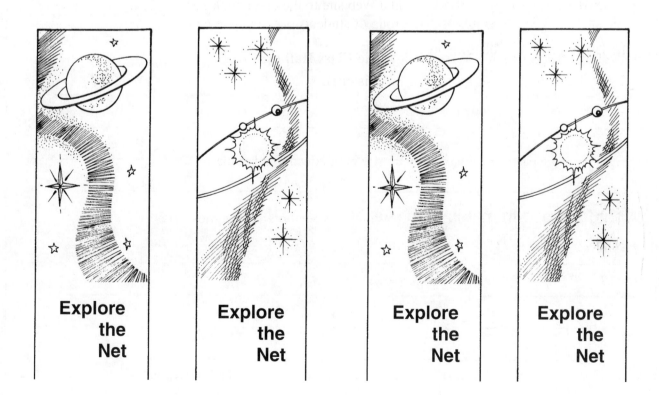

Creating Class Bookmarks (cont.)

Site Name: _____

URL: _____

This site is   **GREAT**   **GOOD**   **OK**

because of the following:

_____

_____

_____

The best part of this site is the following:

_____

_____

_____

What I learned from this Web site:

_____

_____

_____

_____

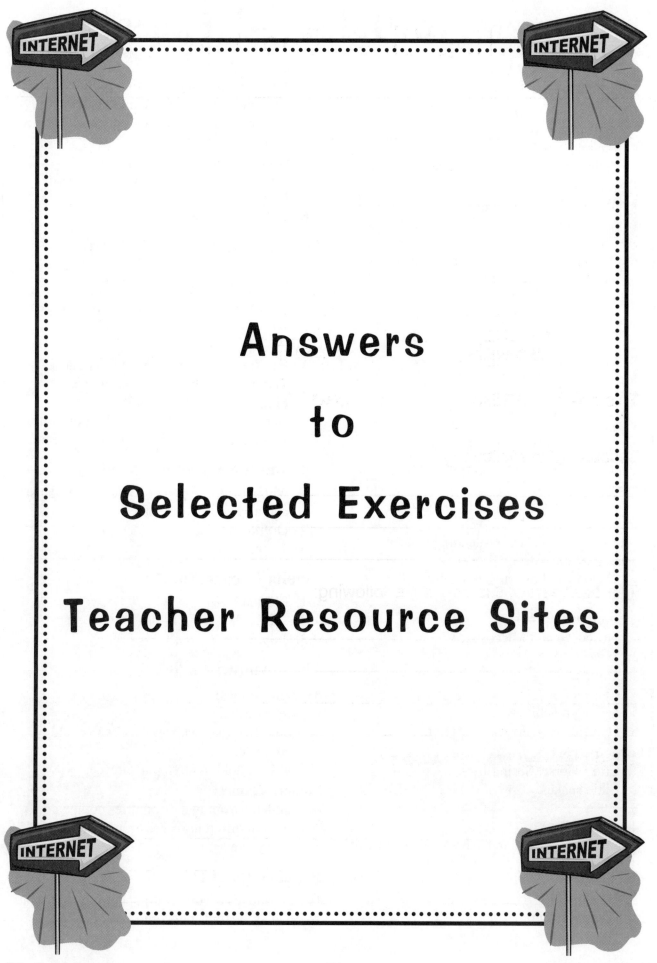

Answers

to

Selected Exercises

Teacher Resource Sites

Answers to Selected Exercises

Native Americans (p. 38)

1. People of the hills
2. One feather would be upright; the other tilted downward
3. He hides in the branches of the largest tree in the woods.
4. All the other birds stop singing
5. Answers may vary
6. The Western Door
7. Onandaga, Oneida, Seneca, Tuscarora, Mohawk, Cayuga

The Pueblos (p.39)

1. Pottery, weaving, jewelry, leather work.
2. The Corn clan, the Turkey clan, the Turquoise clan.
3. Keresan, Tanoan, Spanish.
4. You should:

—treat them with courtesy.

—respect their ways.

—observe posted restrictions.

—watch and listen to dances in silence.

—drive slowly.

—ask permission to photograph residents.

You should not:

—talk to dancers while attending dances.

—applaud once dance is over.

—bring alcohol or drugs to pueblo.

—litter.

The Seminoles (p.40)

1. Muscogee and Miccosukee.
2. Sweetgrass.
3. Turban.
4. Chickee.
5. Sewing machine.
6. Otter, Bear, Wind, Snake, Deer.

The Sioux (p.41)

1. Crazy Horse, Sitting Bull.
2. Little snakes.
3. 1889.
4. dance
5. Indian tacos, Indian fry bread, wojapi (fruit pudding)

Betsy Ross (p. 55)

1. Liberty, freedom, pride.

2. Valor and hardiness; purity and innocence; Vigilance, perseverance and justice.
3. If there's an emergency. It means "Help Me, I am in trouble!"
4. On the back of an envelope.
5. Libya. Over the shores of Tipoli (Fort Derne).
6. 1848, Wisconsin

Alexander Graham Bell (p. 58)

1. Deaf students
2. Thomas Watson
3. "Mr. Watson—Come here—I want to see you."

How the ear hears

1. Ear drum captures sound and vibrates.
2. The bones in the middle ear move.
3. Fluid in the cochlea vibrates.
4. Nerve endings change the vibrations into sound messages and send them to the brain.

A Famous First Flight (p. 65)

1. wings for lift, a power source for propulsion, and a system of control
2. Orville Wright
3. 12 seconds

Amelia Earhart (p. 79)

1. Florida
2. June, 1937
3. July 2, 1937

The Olympics (p. 96)

Ancient Games:

—fewer events.

—only free men who spoke Greek could compete.

—always held in Olympia, Greece.

Modern Games:

—athletes from many countries competed.

—held in different places around the world.

—many events.

Popcorn (p. 101)

1492—Natives tried to sell popcorn to Columbus.

1519—Cortes finds popcorn in Mexico.